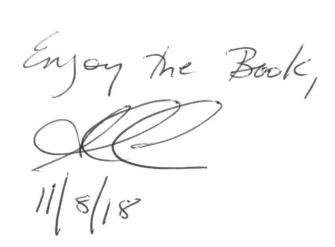

Enjoy the Book,

11/8/18

D1710025

It's Time to Play!

Jack Gardner, Basketball and Kansas State University

It's Time to Play!

Jack Gardner, Basketball and Kansas State University

Steven Michael Farney

ISBN 978-1-58597-435-1
Library of Congress Control Number: 2007928198

LEATHERS
PUBLISHING

4500 College Boulevard
Overland Park, Kansas 66211
888-888-7696
www.leatherspublishing.com

Dedication

This book is dedicated to the memory of Jack Gardner, his Kansas State basketball teams and the many players who wore the purple and white while playing for Coach Gardner at Kansas State College (Kansas State received "university" status in 1959).

"It's Time to Play" is my second in a series of basketball history books about teams in the state of Kansas. My first, **"Title Towns: Class BB Boys Basketball Champions of Kansas,"** was released in September, 2006. Watch for new books in the future. Feel free to contact me at smf2guard@ yahoo.com.

Contents

Acknowledgments

I have been a Kansas State Basketball fan since 1969. In that year, my older brother, Richard, began attended K-State as a freshman. In his weekend trips back to the farm near Wilson, Kansas, he began bringing home "purple" souvenirs for me. He had properly baited the hook! Since Wilson High School (where I was a freshman) also had the colors of purple and white, Kansas State was a perfect fit and it remains a perfect fit to this day.

While attending K-State from 1973-75 and 1976-77, only my interest in Kansas History could match the fondness I had for K-State Basketball. A combination of the two was quite natural and **"It's Time to Play"** is the result.

I want to acknowledge the following people who have helped me on this project:

My oldest brother, Dennis, a loyal KU graduate, who has helped immensely with this book and has always inspired me to write.

My sister-in-law, Peggy Speece Farney, a Nebraska Cornhusker, who also has helped nurture my writing endeavors.

My older brother, Robert, another loyal KU grad, who inspired me to play the game of basketball.

My older brother, Richard, the family's first K-State graduate, who taught me how to play the game of basketball and inspired me to follow him to the Flint Hills.

My parents, Dennis and Agnes Elizabeth Farney, who sacrificed so that their four boys could attend college, no matter the school.

My good friend, Paul Segerson, a Washburn Ichabod, who has helped me research both of my books. By now the Topeka Public Library knows Paul quite well.

My wife, Mary, who has encouraged me to pursue this interest in basketball and history.

My children, Libby, Stephanie and Garrett. At first, they were excited about the stories I was working on. After repeating them for hundreds of times, they now have moved on to new adventures. Secretly, I know they enjoy each book.

The library staff in Salina, Hutchinson, Wichita, Lawrence, Topeka, Manhattan and the Kansas History Museum for their assistance in finding materials about this topic.

The library staff in Ames (Iowa), Lincoln (Nebraska), Norman (Oklahoma), Seattle (Washington), Lexington (Kentucky), and Missoula (Montana) for their help in researching the book.

Tony Crawford and Cindy Von Elling from the Kansas State University Archives.

The University Archives at Iowa State University.

Steve Read and the staff of the McPherson Public Library.

Lorna Nelson and Lenora Lynam from the McPherson County Old Mill Museum (Lindsborg).

Barbara Thomson and the fine staff at Leathers Publishing.

Foreword

The inspiration for this book came from a sports radio call-in show. In 2005, frustrated Kansas State Basketball fans were clamoring for the dismissal of Wildcat Coach Jim Wooldridge. Caller after caller wanted the embattled coach fired and one caller, in particular, struck a nerve with me. He not only wanted "Wooldridge out" but also wanted him to be replaced with a coach "like Jack." When asked by the radio host if "Jack" referred to Jack Hartman (who is the Wildcats' all-time winningest coach), the caller replied, "Is there any other?"

The host didn't respond, but I wanted to: the answer was a resounding YES! There was another Jack, a Jack who put Kansas State Basketball on the map in the first place; a Jack who won league championships and qualified for national tournaments; a Jack who recruited and developed All-American players with regularity; a Jack who became the major antagonist of legendary University of Kansas Coach Phog Allen; a Jack whose fast-paced teams brought basketball interest to a fever pitch on the Manhattan campus; a Jack who became the consummate salesman, lobbying the state to fund the construction of a badly needed field house; a Jack who was quick with a quip and a genuine smile but only until game time; a Jack who had experienced winning and knew what it took to be (and stay) a winner. Yes, there was another Jack. His name was Jack Gardner.

Prior to Gardner's arrival in the summer of 1939, Kansas State had enjoyed limited success in basketball. The school (which played its first game on January 16, 1903) had an overall record of 286 wins and 274 losses in 35 seasons. During that span, the Purple claimed just two conference titles (1917 & 1919) in the old Missouri Valley Conference. Basketball seasons at K-State were feast or famine, a good year followed by several that were not.

Just down the road to the east, the University of Kansas was developing into a consistent basketball power. With head coach Dr. Forrest Clare "Phog" Allen, the Jayhawks began to dominate Kansas State. Arriving in Lawrence in 1919 as head coach, Allen and the Hawks had already fashioned a 42-13 mark against their rivals as the 1939 season ended. Newspapers marveled at the Jayhawks while questioning the Wildcats' commitment to the game. When would K-State get serious about basketball? When would the school in Manhattan decide it was time to play?

Enter Jack Gardner. The 29-year-old coach had always viewed the game as a very serious matter. Arriving in Manhattan, Gardner immediately signaled to the Wildcats that it was time to play, time to challenge for conference titles, time to challenge for national honors. To achieve these goals, Gardner left no stone unturned. Details, no matter how small and seemingly insignificant, did not escape his attention. One example is worth mentioning. In his 1961 book, "Championship Basketball with Jack Gardner," the coach related a story about KU and its big star, Clyde Lovellette. In scouting the Hawks, Gardner and his staff observed that as Lovellette ran down the court, he had a tendency to "look up at the scoreboard and not straight ahead." The K-State coach instructed several of the Wildcats to plant themselves firmly in front of Lovellette, hoping to draw some cheap fouls. They got those fouls and the attention of not only Lovellette but also of the league. With Gardner in Manhattan, things changed in the Flint Hills. This was a "new K-State."

The new Wildcat boss knew that challenging for conference honors more than likely meant going through Phog Allen and the Jayhawks. He met the challenge head-on! Thus, the battles began between the two men and their teams. KU and K-State would clash on the court while the two coaches would carry on their own private feud in the very public media. It became a toss-up as to which was more entertaining: the actual games or the sideshow around those games. One of those sideshows involved an alleged "K-State spy." After a bitter KU defeat to Gardner in 1951, Phog Allen charged that Gardner had placed a Wildcat spy near an open KU locker room window, listening to the halftime words spoken by Allen. That very "detective" was later seen sitting on the Wildcat bench in the second half. To Allen, that was evidence enough of a crime. As the two teams prepared to battle again, this time in Manhattan, Gardner was asked about the incident and Allen's assessment. "I have no idea what he is talking about," replied Gardner, "and I doubt very seriously he knows himself what he is talking about!" The K-State coach won this verbal skirmish, but Allen had more than one moment where he put the "boy wonder from Manhattan" in his place! Sports writers loved every minute.

There were few dull moments when KU and K-State clashed on the court. Gardner's first teams unsuccessfully challenged the Hawks but then began to win quite regularly. The young coach was innovative, unconventional and unafraid to experiment with new offensive schemes and defenses. The games were high-stakes contests, often with conference titles on the line. At that time, only the winner of the conference could advance in post-season play. For all the other conference teams, no title meant "time to check-in the uniforms." With the stakes so high, emotions between the two schools were never more intense. After years of KU dominance, a real rivalry was born.

The other conference games were battles as well. Gardner would more than win his share of contests. He was a master at scouting and preparation and his teams were ready to play, no matter the talent level he possessed. It would be a hallmark of all of Gardner's teams. In his later years as coach at the University of Utah, *Sports Illustrated* commented that "Gardner could win with an old maid in the post and four midgets!" The Big Six (soon to become the Big Seven) learned this first-hand.

When I was interviewed about my first book, **"Title Towns: Class BB Boys Basketball Champions of Kansas,"** I stated that I liked to research Kansas teams and towns, players and coaches who may have been forgotten with time. The Jack Gardner era at Kansas State seems to fit that criteria. Wildcat fans are very knowledgeable about Cat stars Ernie Barrett and Dick Knostman, two of the great Gardner players whose jerseys now hang from the rafters in Bramlage Coliseum. Wildcat fans are also aware of the two Final Four teams (1948 & 1951) that were coached by Gardner. But what is remembered about Clarence Brannum, Jack Horacek, Chris Langvardt, Rick Harman or Jack Stone? What is remembered about "Ivy" Jim Iverson, Howie Shannon, Dan Howe, Gene "The Jet" Wilson, David Weatherby or a host of other players coached by Gardner? What is remembered about Gardner's 1940 team, his first, or the 1953 team, his last? What role did World War II have to play in Gardner's coaching career? All are part of the Kansas State Basketball story and that story is told here.

Using game summaries, newspaper articles, pictures and statistics, this book details the Jack Gardner days at Kansas State: the wins, the losses, the disappointments, the conference titles, the national tournaments, the controversies and the newspaper bombshells. Kansas State has been blessed to have two "Jacks" as head basketball coaches but the first was Jack Gardner. It was Gardner who awoke Kansas State from a deep basketball slumber and boldly announced, "It's Time to Play!"

Steven Farney
April, 2007

1940
New Man On Campus

Record: 6-12
Conference Record: 2-8 (t-4ᵗʰ)

Team Captain: Ernie Miller

Ernie Miller   Joe Robertson   Jack Horacek   Ervin Reid

Norris Holstrom   Frank Woolf   Melvin Seelye

Kenny Graham   Chris Langravdt   D.S. Guerrant

Who's the new guy? If Kansas State students couldn't recognize the new basketball face on campus in the fall of 1939, they weren't alone. No, Wildcat fans knew the names and faces of the four returning lettermen: Ervin Reid, Melvin Seelye, Joe Robertson and Ernie Miller. The new "guy" was not a player. He was actually the new Wildcat basketball coach, Jack Gardner.

At 29-years-old, Gardner was the youngest coach at any major university or college in the country. A star forward, four-year letterman and captain and MVP on the 1932 University of Southern California team, the youthful Gardner looked more like a player than a coach. Yet in his limited years of head coaching experience, Gardner was not limited in basketball success. On the contrary, he was already a proven winner.

After completing his playing days at USC in 1932, Gardner pursued his Master's degree and assisted Trojan basketball coach Sam Barry. While assisting Barry, Gardner also coached the Los Angeles Athletic basketball team to the Southern Pacific AAU Championship. In 1933, once graduate school was complete, Gardner landed his first head coaching job at Alhambra, California, High School. In two seasons, Alhambra posted a record of 29-11 and won two championships. In 1935, Gardner moved to Modesto Junior College. There, the young coach won three successive state titles in four seasons. His Modesto teams recorded an overall record of 83-27 during that time. The Gardner reputation grew, not only in California, but far beyond the United States. Twice Gardner traveled to Japan at the behest of the Japanese government and conducted basketball clinics.

As Gardner arrived in Manhattan in 1939, the Wildcats would quickly be given a crash course in his basketball philosophy. To be successful on the court, Gardner knew the Cats had to dominate every inch of the court. Defensively, the team would be tenacious and aggressive, relying on speed at each and every opportunity. Gardner knew that consistent (and persistent) defensive pressure not only demoralized opponents but also created offensive opportunities. These offensive chances many times would carry the team through rough nights when "the shots just wouldn't fall." Good defense first and foremost came from within a player's heart. Gardner quickly set out to change the Wildcats' hearts and convince his new team on the value of defensive basketball and the many rewards that could be derived from that defense.

Offensively, Gardner's teams used speed to get up and down the court. The young coach felt that an up-tempo game was not only more enjoyable to watch, but was also more enjoyable to play. With a faster pace, all players became part of the action and Gardner did not want scoring chances limited to just the forward and center positions. Rather, he wanted all five players to be scoring threats and the fast break gave each their opportunities. Opponents, fearing the fast break, many times changed their offensive mannerisms to protect against it. This was just another benefit of playing faster. Speed went hand-in-hand with conditioning and Gardner's Wildcats would be superbly conditioned. Great attention was spent on diet and proper rest. Gardner's pre-game meal of tea and toast was initially met with some resistance from the Cats, but they soon learned that the young coach knew of what he spoke. Tea and toast it would be!

This was the basketball identity that Gardner brought to the K-State campus. He would need all of his skills and experience when he arrived in the Flint Hills in the summer of '39. Since the inception of the Big Six (1929), the highest conference finish for K-State was a tie for third. The

Cats last had a winning season in 1931. The 1939 team endured a 5-13 campaign. Star athletes steered clear of Manhattan. Other schools had more promise, more prestige. Gardner had known nothing but success. Perhaps in Manhattan he would finally meet his match. The young coach was undaunted. He had more than enough confidence for the entire school of 4,090 students. First and foremost, attitudes had to change. Kansas State had become too comfortable with losing games. Gardner preached an entirely different message: that was the old Kansas State basketball. It didn't reside in Manhattan anymore!

Baker (Manhattan): The Wildcats opened the season with a 35-33 upset victory over Baker College. It was a triumphant debut for Gardner, but certainly not in the beginning. Baker, which was favored to win the game by as much as 15 points, jumped to a 21-5 lead after just 12 minutes of action and appeared primed to run K-State right out of Nichols Gymnasium. The Cats clawed back and cut the deficit to 25-14 at halftime. The K-State rally began in earnest in the second half. The Wildcats finally gained their first lead with just one minute to play on a long shot by Topeka sophomore, Jack Horacek. Joe Robertson added a free throw late in the contest to clinch Gardner's first victory at K-State. Ernie Miller led the Cats in scoring with 12 points while Kenneth Poppe netted 12 for Baker. Gardner, the 10th coach in Kansas State history, joined six other Wildcat coaches in successfully winning his first career game.

Doane College (Manhattan): Kansas State grabbed their second victory in as many starts as they defeated Doane College (Crete, Nebraska), 46-28. It was a much easier win for the Cats but the game was extremely rough. All told, 33 fouls were whistled in the contest, 21 in the first half. Although Kansas State played much better than in the Baker game, the Cats managed a slim 18-12 lead at the intermission. Still, K-State had to feel very good: they had a six-point lead even after missing nine free throw attempts in the first half. Doane cut the lead to 26-21 early in the second half before the Cats closed with a 20-7 push to get the win. Ervin Reid (13) and Robertson (10) led the scoring efforts.

K-State embarked on their first road trip, a two-game slate against Colorado State College in Ft. Collins. As the team prepared to leave, Gardner set down some new guidelines. One in particular caught the player's attention. Gardner insisted that all players strictly watch their diets while on the road. No longer would there be unlimited trips to the food cart! It was becoming crystal clear: basketball was a serious matter to the new coach. The players would be wise to think the same.

Colorado State (Ft. Collins): Kansas State got off on the right foot as they edged Colorado State, 42-36, in their first road game of the season. Colorado State was a sophomore-dominated squad that figured to become quite good as the season progressed. They struggled against the Wildcats, however, especially in the first half. K-State jumped to a 17-6 lead at halftime as the home team managed just one field goal in the entire half. Colorado State awoke in the second stanza, and if not for the nine points scored by Joe Robertson, K-State might have lost the game. Miller led the scoring with 10 points while Robertson nailed nine, all in the second half.

Colorado State (Ft. Collins): Just one night later the two teams met again, but this time with much different results. Colorado State trimmed the Cats, 52-44, to split the two-game series. K-State held a 25-24 lead at the half as Colorado State played with much more precision than they displayed in the first game. As the second half began, the Cats scored five straight points and seemed poised to dash to victory. The home boys had other intentions, however, and led by Bus Bergman, began to hit from all angles. Dan Howe, the Wildcat forward from Stockdale, kept the Cats close. Howe managed 10 points in the second half but the Purple never could regain the lead. Bergman ended the game with 12 points to lead Colorado State while Howe (14) and Miller (10) led the Cats.

K-State returned to Manhattan for a shortened Christmas break before embarking on another road trip, this time to Evansville and Kentucky. Overall, Gardner was quite pleased with his team and also enjoyed something new during the holidays: it was his first white Christmas!

Evansville (Evansville): Kansas State displayed great skill and tenacity but lost to Evansville College, 38-32. The Purple Aces jumped to a 19-10 lead at the half and seemed in complete control before the Cats rallied. K-State trimmed the lead to 33-32 with just four minutes to play and not only had the momentum but also had the ball. They couldn't find the nets, however, and Evansville drifted away to their fifth straight win. Howe led the Cats with nine points while Reid added eight.

Kentucky (Lexington): K-State was clearly outclassed as Kentucky destroyed the Cats, 53-26. The Kentucky team, led by guards Mickey Rouse and Lee Huber, quickly pounced on the Wildcats, holding them to just two field goals the entire first half! As the teams left the court at halftime, K-State trailed 32-7. The score was only half of the beating. Ernie Miller, starting senior guard and captain, suffered a broken jaw and was taken to a Lexington hospital. Gardner now was faced with the prospect of sophomores Howe, Horacek, Ted Garrett and D.S. Guerrant playing much more prominent roles on the team.

In the second half, Kentucky coaching legend (and Kansas native) Adolph Rupp called off the dogs, and the teams played even to the final horn. Richard Checksfield led the Cats in scoring with seven points. K-State boarded the train for the return to Manhattan while Miller remained hospitalized in Lexington. He would return to Manhattan on a later date.

Oklahoma (Manhattan): Before 3,000 students jammed into Nichols Gymnasium, the Cats opened the Big Six campaign, losing to Oklahoma, 50-33. The Sooners, one of the favorites in the conference, were in the foulest of moods as they came to Manhattan. KU had just manhandled Oklahoma in Lawrence, 46-26. The Hawks dominated the two star players of Oklahoma, Jim McNatt and Marvin Mesch, holding them to just three points. The two were keys to Coach Bruce Drake's fast-paced offensive. In 1939, the "run-run" Sooners averaged 46.2 points/game, a Big Six Conference record. The speed used by the Sooners was a fan favorite and the team was dubbed the "Boy Scats." KU had bottled-up McNatt and Mesch and if K-State hoped to have any chance, that would be the Purple game plan as well. The Cats did a marvelous job on the two Sooner stars early in the game. K-State trailed by just four, 19-15, as the teams reached halftime.

The boys on the bench await the nod from Coach Gardner.
— Courtesy of Kansas State University Archives

The southern visitors took over in the second half and OU pulled away quite easily. McNatt (12) and Herb Scheffler (10) found double figures for the Sooners. Scheffler also did a defensive number on Ervin Reid, holding him to just five tallies. Robertson (eight) and Horacek (seven) paced the Cats.

Long before anyone had heard of the "R.P.I." or "strength of schedule," a similar version was published in early January, 1940. An East Coast organization had reduced basketball to a mathematical equation by a system called "the average power index of opposition." By a series of calculations, this organization published a number which ranked the strength of teams across the country. A score of 1.000 was perfection. The University of Southern California had the highest number and was therefore considered the top team in the land. Listed below were the power rankings of the Big Six teams:

Kansas	.245
Oklahoma	.241
Iowa State	.236
Nebraska	.219
Missouri	.205
Kansas State	.195

Gardner was somewhat amused by the system. Everyone kept placing K-State last. As the Cats prepared for a road trip to play DePaul and Creighton, Gardner hoped both schools believed in "the average power index of opposition" and practiced accordingly!

DePaul (Chicago): K-State found few positives as DePaul easily defeated the Cats, 56-30. The game was part of a double-header. Later in the evening, KU defeated Loyolla of Chicago, 46-36, as Ralph Miller nailed 22 points in the Hawk victory. K-State was not so fortunate. DePaul jumped to a 5-0 lead and never trailed, although Horacek led a brief rally to cut the deficit to just 19-16 at the half. There would be no second-half magic as DePaul easily pulled away. Stan Szukala and Elmer Gainor led DePaul with 13 and 11 points respectively, while Horacek led K-State with nine. The Wildcats immediately boarded a train for Omaha and a date with Creighton. K-State had first played Creighton in 1925, and since that date, the two teams had met five times. The Bluejays had won them all.

Creighton (Omaha): In a surprising upset, K-State defeated Creighton 50-44 to stop the five-game losing streak. Reid and Robertson were the keys. The two combined for 16 first-half points as the Cats opened a 24-13 lead at the intermission. In the second half, the Bluejays twice cut the deficit to five points but K-State had all the answers to claim the victory. Reid led all scorers with 16 points, followed closely by Robertson with 12. No Bluejay scored in double figures. The Cats returned to Manhattan and had several days of preparation for THE RIVAL: KU! K-State had lost four straight to the Hawks. Their last victory had been on February 11, 1937. Gardner knew the significance of the game. His preparation was intense and secretive.

Kansas (Lawrence): In Gardner's first encounter with Phog Allen, K-State was nipped by the Jayhawks, 34-33. It was the 91st meeting between the two schools (the first game being played on January 25, 1907). KU had claimed 59 of those games. On this night, they would narrowly claim number 60! More than 3,000 fans (and Governor Payne Ritner) crammed into Hoch Auditorium to watch the game. K-State jumped to an early 15-9 lead before KU's Bob Allen (Phog's son) and Bruce Voran keyed a 10-0 run to claim a 19-15 Jayhawk lead at the half. In the second half, there were numerous ties, the last being 33-33 with less than three minutes remaining. Both teams had several chances to break the deadlock but neither scored until Voran was fouled by Frank Woolf with just four seconds remaining. The Jayhawk guard missed his first charity toss, but netted the second. The Cats could not get off a shot and lost the heartbreaker, their fifth straight loss to KU. Allen and Voran both netted 10 points each to lead KU while Reid paced the Cats with nine. KU fans, excited to have escaped the contest with a win, rushed the floor to congratulate the victors but one pretty coed showed her excitement another way. She raced straight to Phog Allen himself and planted a kiss squarely on the jaw of the legend. Allen was speechless about the incident but his smile spoke volumes about the win.

Even in defeat, the game demonstrated one of Jack Gardner's greatest coaching talents: strategy. The new Wildcat mentor concocted a defensive plan against the Hawks. Gardner had four of his players play man-to-man defense while Ervin Reid was positioned in the center of the lane. Reid operated similarly to a hockey goalie, moving freely within his area, blocking shots, grabbing rebounds and deflecting passes. Reid guarded no one in particular. In fact, for the entire game, one KU player was unguarded and only became a concern if he approached the basket. Melvin Seelye drew the unenviable assignment of being Ralph Miller's shadow, and shadow Miller he did: the KU star managed just seven points, well below his average.

The defense was new to the Big Six, but not new in the world of basketball. Gardner had learned the strategy from legendary coach Bob Johnson, who had used the defense while coaching at Wichita University and Kansas Wesleyan College in Salina. There was a key difference, however. Johnson had instructed his four players to play a zone defense while Gardner had them play man-to-man. These variations would become a hallmark of Gardner's squads. Opponents were never quite certain what the innovative coach would dream up next.

Nebraska (Manhattan): The Cats claimed their first Big Six win with a 32-25 victory over Nebraska. The game time had to be moved up one-half hour to allow students to decorate Nichols Gymnasium for a military ball the next night! Area newspapers had a field day with the decorations, wondering when Kansas State would get serious, build a new field house and give Wildcat basketball the respect it needed.

The Cornhuskers were the tallest team in the conference, with all of their starters taller than 6'0". Al Randall, their imposing center, was 6'7". Despite the size disadvantage, K-State was in control from the opening minutes, jumping to a 18-13 lead at the half. The Cats stretched the lead to 30-20 before Nebraska managed a late rally to cut the deficit. Randall led NU with nine points, while Horacek had nine to lead the Cats. K-State got the win and the dance decorations were put in place. It was a win-win for everyone!

Iowa State (Manhattan): K-State grabbed their second straight conference victory, edging Iowa State 29-28. The Cyclones were winless in the conference, but hardly played that way. The game was tight from the outset, with the Cats holding a narrow 13-12 lead at the half. Late in the final period, that lead grew to 25-18 before Iowa State mounted a furious rally and cut the margin to just one, 27-26, with one minute remaining. A key bucket by Horacek pushed the lead back to three and the Cats withstood a final desperation heave by the Cyclones to notch a one-point victory. With the win, K-State vaulted into fourth place in the conference while Iowa State sank deeper into the cellar. Reid and Horacek led the scoring for the Wildcats with six points each.

The two straight conference wins did not go unnoticed. Kansas State fans across the state were excited at what the young coach had accomplished in such rapid time. Gardner was constructing something in Manhattan and some aptly named the young coach "Jack the Builder." If Gardner could put together a competitive team so quickly, fans began to clamor for the next step: a new field house! Nichols, affectionately nicknamed "The Cracker Box Coliseum," couldn't possibly hold the enthusiasm that Gardner and his Wildcats had generated. For his part, Gardner did little to quell the excitement but he remained focused on the games ahead. Wins and losses were something he could control. Gardner valued the advice and counsel of his former coach, Sam Barry, and the new Wildcat boss kept in weekly contact with him via amateur radio.

Oklahoma (Norman): Kansas State lost to conference-leading Oklahoma, 34-29, in a bruising contest before 4,500 fans in Norman. The Sooners played without star Marvin Mesch (illness) and were hampered, not only by his absence, but by the Wildcat defense. The Cats gave a splendid effort but hurt their chances by poor foul shooting. K-State trailed throughout the game but rallied late in the contest to tie the game at 28-28. OU rattled off four-straight points and grabbed the victory. Reid (nine) and Chris Langvardt (seven) led the K-State scoring.

It was the most physical contest of the year and by far the costliest: four Wildcats were seriously injured. Robertson (ankle), Reid (shoulder), Seelye (leg) and Langvardt (knee) all were sent to the sidelines, several with possible season-ending injuries. With four of the five starters shelved, Gardner had to reach deep into his bag of tricks to field a competitive squad.

Missouri (Manhattan): With four starters playing sparingly, the Cats were manhandled by Missouri, 44-28. It was evident very early in the game that Robertson, Reid, Seelye and Langvardt were greatly missed. The Tigers jumped to an early lead and widened it to a 27-12 halftime advantage. The 2,800 fans, hardly impressed with the first half action, entertained themselves at halftime. Several students paraded around the floor with a huge banner that read "We Want a New Field House." The banner drew thunderous cheers in the tiny gymnasium. The second half was much better. The Cats held MU scoreless for nearly 12 minutes and crawled closer before the Tigers regained their shooting touch and pulled away for the victory. Horacek led K-State in scoring with 10 points while Langvardt, struggling with a knee injury, added nine. With the loss the Cats saw their conference record fall to 2-4.

K-State did receive some good news on the injury front. Ernie Miller, out since the Kentucky game with a broken jaw, was cleared to play. Unfortunately, Miller sprained his ankle during the last practice and would be lost for another two to three weeks. Miller had to feel cursed. Gardner was beginning to feel cursed himself.

Iowa State (Ames): The wheels of defeat kept rolling for the Cats, as they were defeated by Iowa State, 45-32. It was a poor effort against a Cyclone team that had been winless in the conference. Reid played sparingly and Robertson was still sidelined as the Wildcats struggled from about every aspect imaginable. Langvardt and Horacek each netted 11 points to lead the Cat scoring. Gordon Nicholas, the Cyclones star center, nailed 17 points to lead all scorers.

Nebraska (Lincoln): Kansas State continued their swoon as Nebraska blasted the Cats, 61-28. As K-State saw starters injured and residing on the bench, the Cornhuskers welcomed back starters Don Fitz and Harry Pitcaithley, both of whom had been injured. The two players inspired NU but Frank Tallman, the Nebraska forward, carried the team. Tallman scored 23 points in the game as the Purple had no answer for his abilities. Norris Holstrom paced the Cats efforts with eight points. With the win, Nebraska tied K-State for fourth in the conference with identical 2-6 records.

Missouri (Columbia): The Cats lost their fifth consecutive conference game as Missouri raced to a 36-23 victory. It was a key win for the Tigers. They improved their conference record to 7-1 and remained in striking distance with both KU and OU for the conference title. For the Cats, it was more of the same. Injuries limited minutes for key players and the Wildcats could not overcome the absences. They did keep it close, however, trailing only 16-12 at the half. It was still a three-point game (22-19) late in the second half when the Tigers kicked into high gear for the win. Langvardt led the Cats with seven points while Clay Cooper nailed 13 to lead Missouri.

Kansas (Manhattan): Kansas State closed out the 1940 season with a 44-33 loss to the Kansas Jayhawks. Robertson and Reid did not play due to their injuries and Dan Howe was an academic casualty as well. Clearly out-manned, K-State kept the game close and withstood two significant Jayhawk runs and still only trailed by four (22-18) as halftime arrived. KU pulled away in the second half as Ralph Miller scored 14 points to lead the Hawks. Horacek led all scorers with 16 points as the Cats ended the season with a 2-8 conference mark, and an overall record of 6-12. Horacek and Holstrom were Honorable-Mention selections by the Big Six as KU, MU and OU tied for the conference title with identical 8-2 records. In a playoff, Oklahoma defeated Missouri 52-41 but lost to the Hawks 45-39. With that victory, KU advanced to the national tournament and finished second to Indiana, losing to the Hoosiers in the championship game.

With the basketball season complete in Manhattan, Gardner immediately hit the ground running. First, he attended the Class A State High School Basketball Tournament in Topeka to survey the talent. Two players stood out above the rest: Ray Evans of Wyandotte and Gerald Tucker of Winfield. In the coming years, both Evans and Tucker would give the Cats "fits," but Tucker's impact on Kansas State would also be in a rather unusual manner!

Students hang from rafters during the Missouri game — Courtesy of Kansas State University Archives

Second, Gardner became actively involved in the drive to build a new field house. A public campaign was launched on April 16, 1940 to gather 4,000 signatures of students, townspeople and K-State fans in support of a new facility. A beautiful scale model was unveiled of one possible design. The structure would seat 9,000 fans and would include a pool, separate gymnasium and removable basketball flooring so that football, baseball and track practices could be held indoors. Joe Robertson, a starter for the Basketball Cats, served as the student chairman of the Field House Committee. Gardner spoke at the opening rally and as he traveled the state on recruiting trips, continued to spread the word. On April 30, the two-week campaign culminated with a "mock" cornerstone being laid at the proposed field house site located just north of the football stadium. With trumpets blaring (literally), Mike Ahearn, Athletics Director, laid the stone in place. On the next day, the student committee met personally with Governor Payne Ritner at the Statehouse to present him with the petition and 4,000 signatures. Ritner was not unsympathetic to the cause. "I agree perfectly as to the need for the building," said the governor. "It is my hope that it is one of the first new structures to be approved for Kansas State." The effort generated plenty of media attention but everyone knew one thing would make or break this project: money! That would continue to be the main issue the state would wrestle with.

The 1940 season would not be completed without a word from KU Coach, Phog Allen. Allen had long felt that the college game was somewhat "dull" due to low team scoring. The KU skipper proposed that a smaller ball be used, which would certainly increase the scoring efforts. Although many coaches shared Allen's sentiments, his suggestion of new basketballs appeared a bit too draconian. Money was always in short supply and with each day's newspaper came ominous stories from both Europe and Asia. America was uneasy as armed conflict inched closer to the U.S. mainland. How long would those problems remain over there? Before any basketball changes could be made, serious thought and testing were needed.

Missouri Mathematics Professor George Edwards decided to add his "two-cents" to the issue. The MU professor conducted an experiment. Edwards had 14 players shoot a total of 3,500 shots (250 for each man) at a standard-sized rim (18") and then had the same players shoot a total of 3,500 shots at a larger rim (20"). The results: 2,017 baskets were made on the larger rim while 1,731 shots were made on the standard-sized rim. What did it prove? Not enough to warrant any equipment changes. Perhaps Missouri had proven something, however. The Tigers were not going to let Phog Allen claim to be the only basketball innovator around the Big Six!

Team Statistics (Newspaper box scores):

K-State:	605 points	33.6/game
Opponents:	741 points	41.1/game

Individual Scoring Leaders (Newspaper box scores):

Ervin Reid (Manhattan, Ks.)	100 points	6.7/game
Jack Horacek (Topeka, Ks.)	96 points	5.6/game
Chris Langvardt (Alta Vista, Ks.)	67 points	4.5/game
Melvin Seelye (Ft. Scott, Ks.)	66 points	3.9/game
Joe Robertson (Brownstone, Ind.)	60 points	4.6/game
Norris Holstrom (Topeka, Ks.)	53 points	3.1/game
Dan Howe (Stockdale, Ks.)	52 points	4.3/game
Ernie Miller (Independence, Ks.)	36 points	5.1/game
Richard Checksfield (Topeka, Ks.)	27 points	4.5/game
Ted Garrett (Shawnee Mission, Ks.)	19 points	3.2/game
Kenny Graham (Framington, Mass.)	11 points	1.0/game
Others	18 points	

NCAA CHAMPION: Indiana (20-3)
RUNNER-UP: Kansas
THIRD PLACE: Duquesne & Southern California

1941
Sardines in the Cracker Box

Record: 6-12
Conference Record: 3-7 (5th)

Team Captain: Norris Holstrom

Lettermen — Back row: George Mendenhall, Dean Lill, Tony Guy, Ken Graham. Front row: Capt. Norris Holstrom, Chris Langvardt, Danny Howe, Jack Horacek. Larry Beaumont is not in the picture.
— Courtesy of Kansas State University Archives

As the 1941 basketball season approached in Manhattan, it would have been difficult to create more excitement among K-State fans. Despite a 6-12 season and the departure of six lettermen from the '40 squad, Wildcat fans were energized. The Cats, with their emphasis on speed and pressure defense, were fun to watch and the basketball future was promising, not only in 1941, but seemingly for years to come. K-State returned four lettermen: Chris Langvardt (also a key member of the football team), Jack Horacek, Norris Holstrom and Kenny Graham. In addition, Dan Howe (who had some eligibility problems in '40) was expected to make a major contribution, as were Larry Beaumont, Tony Guy, George Mendenhall and Dean Lill. Oh yes, Kansas State also returned one other key element: Jack Gardner himself!

In his first season, the young mentor had made a lasting impression, not only on Cat loyalists, but on coaches around the country. Off the court, Gardner was a bright, energetic and friendly. People genuinely liked his company and the media took note and nicknamed him "Genial Jack." On the court, however, he was the fiercest of competitors. "Genial Jack" studied his opponents under a microscope, observing the smallest of details. Weak links would be exploited to the fullest degree. Kansas State opponents had grown accustomed to the "old K-State," a school they respected but beat quite regularly. "The "new K-State" frankly was threatening the old order.

Gardner was a consummate salesman for all that was good about Kansas State. His confidence and enthusiasm were unmatched and sometimes appeared brash to others outside of the Wildcat circle. This persona won him few friends amongst the other coaches, but Gardner was not in Manhattan to win friends. He came to the Flint Hills to win games and win them quickly. He was a no-nonsense coach and his players would follow the lead. Basketball had always been a serious venture to the young man. He expected it to be a serious venture in Manhattan and to any "non-believers," Gardner preached a message of conversion. Like him or not, Gardner was above all an innovative coach and he had demonstrated this in his first season with the Wildcats. The rest of the conference took notice. Opposing coaches knew that if Gardner's recruiting ever caught up with his coaching talents, the Big Six would get a steady diet of the new Kansas State!

In 1940, it appeared Gardner's recruiting had already caught hold. Long before basketball fans had heard of a "Fab Five," newspapers proclaimed Gardner's 1940 recruiting class the "Dream Team." The young coach had landed five incredible prizes: Gerald Tucker of Winfield, Dale Covert of El Dorado, Cliff Sickles of Winfield, Don Coulter of Arkansas City and John Bortka of Kansas City. For years, Wildcat basketball fans across the state had bemoaned the fact that great in-state talent seemed to migrate everywhere but Manhattan. In one short year, Gardner had corralled five of the most celebrated gems and had them all in the Flint Hills!

Getting them to Manhattan proved to be the easiest part. Keeping them there was another story. Before the leaves had fallen from the trees, Sickles, Coulter and Covert left school for various reasons. The biggest shock, however, came on November 9: Tucker also was leaving Manhattan. He was considered the finest prospect that the state had produced since KU grabbed Howard Engleman from Arkansas City. The young star left K-State and then surfaced as a student at the University of Oklahoma. The reasons for his departure appeared to be many but one reported incident took on an almost comical nature. Tucker's K-State fraternity house discovered a small fire one evening. A neighboring fraternity, ignoring the fire, instead paraded in front of the burning house with mock seriousness carrying a hastily lettered sign that read:

"Save Tucker first. To hell with the women and children!" The incident reportedly irritated the Winfield star. Whatever the reason, "Titanic Tuck" was gone and he was a huge loss. K-State viewed Tucker as a steppingstone to a possible conference championship and perhaps even a new field house. Gardner was so impressed with the athletic talents of the Winfield native that he said, "You see a boy of his talent once a decade!" Now, Tucker would be donning the colors of Oklahoma. Freshmen were not eligible for the varsity in 1941 and Tucker would bide his time. When the 1942 season dawned, there would be plenty of fireworks amongst the Big Six family. Those fireworks would center around Tucker! Gardner, for his part, diplomatically expressed disappointment in the young man's decision and turned his attention to 1941. Add two more talents to his list of many: Gardner was resilient. He could adapt.

Pep Students yell for a fieldhouse.
— Courtesy of Kansas State University Archives

Washburn (Manhattan): On December 6, K-State opened the season with a 23-15 victory over Washburn. The game marked the first time the two had met since the 1936 season, when the Cats won twice. The contest was a personal one for the Wildcats' Jack Horacek and Norris Holstrom. They were matched against their former Topeka High teammates, Eugene Lane and Dennis Payne. All had been members of the 1937 Trojan team.

K-State led 12-5 at halftime. The Ichabods cut the lead to four points early in the second half, before Horacek netted three quick points. Washburn drew no closer. Tony Guy (eight) led the Cats in scoring while Horacek, Beaumont and Mendenhall each added four.

The game was the usual sellout at Nichols, and at halftime the cheerleaders paraded around the court, carrying a sign that read "We Want a Crackerjack Field House, Instead of a Cracker Box Gymnasium!" The drive to fund a new field house was slowly gaining momentum with each Wildcat victory.

Washburn (Topeka): In a quick rematch, the Cats defeated Washburn, 33-29, this time in Whiting Fieldhouse in Topeka. The Ichabods had a polished effort in the first half and led 23-16. K-State began to chip away at the lead in the second half and narrowed the deficit to 25-22 when Washburn guard Chuck Ostmeyer was nailed for his fourth foul. It was an opportunity the Cats could exploit and they quickly tied the game, 26-26. Washburn regrouped and gained the lead, 29-28, with just three minutes to play, but two errant passes led to easy scores by Horacek as the Cats pulled ahead. Washburn was held scoreless the final three minutes as K-State gained their second victory. Each team nailed 11 field goals in the contest, but K-State turned 14 Washburn fouls into 11 points at the line. The Cats were 11 of 17 from the charity stripe while the Ichabods were seven of 10. That difference was just enough. Horacek had a brilliant game, leading all scorers with 15 points. Beaumont and Dan Howe each added four.

Doane College (Manhattan): The Cats cruised to their third victory of the young season, this time defeating Doane College, 54-27. Doane enjoyed its last lead at 9-8, but it was all K-State from there. The Cats powered ahead, fueled by an 18-1 run, and held a commanding 26-10 lead at the half. Doane never challenged again. Guy led all scorers with 14 points while Horacek (13) and Howe (12) also netted double figures.

Things now got much more difficult: Next on the schedule was the Kentucky Wildcats, coached by Kansas native Adolph Rupp. At the start of the 1940 campaign, the Wildcats from the Bluegrass State had plastered K-State in Lexington, 53-26. They returned several key players from that 16-5 team and were expected to be a great challenge again. Rupp was already a coaching legend. Kentucky had captured five Southeastern Conference Championships under Rupp and he sported a 163-26 record in just ten seasons in Lexington. Kentucky was led by Lee Huber, a senior guard who was a strong candidate for All-American honors.

Kentucky (Manhattan): In a tremendous effort, K-State narrowly lost to Kentucky, 28-25. The game was played before the usual packed house and the fans were on the edge of their seats the entire contest. It was the most polished Cat performance of the season except for one small detail: free throws! K-State managed just 11 of 21 from the charity stripe and that proved very costly in the end.

Kentucky held a slim 16-13 lead at the half as the visitors from Lexington completely bottled up Horacek (he managed just five points in the game). Tony Guy made up the difference, however, and single-handedly kept the Purple close. K-State trailed 27-22 late in the game when Holstrom converted a three-point-play. Kentucky went into a delay game and K-State never had any real opportunity to gain the lead. The visitors escaped with the three-point victory. Guy led K-State in scoring with 11 points. Holstrom added six.

Banners and signs were nearly everywhere in Nichols, all urging the students to visit with their parents, friends and state legislators about the urgent need to build a new field house. One banner captured the student's sentiment perfectly: "2,800 Seats, 4,100 Students: Are we Sardines?"

The Cats would enjoy a very short Christmas break as they prepared to travel east for four games. They were joined by Chris Langvardt, who had played in the '40 season and was a Wildcat football star as well. Langvardt had suffered a shoulder injury in the pigskin season and required surgery, but he was fit to travel with the team as they boarded the train for the East Coast. Stops would include games against Villanova, George Washington, Seton Hall and Illinois.

Villanova (Philadelphia): The traveling Wildcats were hardily in polished form as Villanova easily defeated them, 51-34. K-State trailed 20-9 at the half and seemed to have left their game "on the train." For the undefeated Villanova Wildcats, it was their eighth straight win of the new season. Horacek, Howe and Langvardt led the scoring for K-State as each nailed six points.

George Washington (Washington, D.C.): K-State continued to struggle on the road trip and lost to the George Washington Colonials, 48-25. The contest was a "slick" affair, but not in terms of execution. The game was "slick" because the gymnasium floor had just been treated for an upcoming dance! Neither team could gain any traction and early on it was unclear if either team would ever score. The Colonials broke the scoring ice and finally split the nets with five minutes gone in the contest. K-State remained scoreless for nearly 10 minutes and that drought was, for all practical purposes, the game. The Colonials led 24-8 at the half and were never threatened. Howe and Guy led the Cats in scoring with five points each.

Seton Hall (South Orange): K-State's road woes continued as the Cats lost to Seton Hall, 34-29. For the third straight game, K-State played tentatively in the first half and quickly fell behind 22-13 at the intermission. They did manage a good comeback, however, but it was not enough to prevent Seton Hall from winning its 31st straight home game. Beaumont led the Cats in scoring with nine points, while Guy added eight.

Illinois (Champaign): Kansas State concluded the four-game road trip, losing to Illinois 45-29. The Cats jumped to an early 12-9 lead when Illinois Coach Doug Mills made some strategic changes: he inserted the starters! Mills had withheld his usual starting crew but as K-State began to gain some real momentum, he inserted the five with immediate results. The Cats managed just one more point and trailed 22-13 at the half. The margin quickly grew in the second half as K-State fell for the fifth straight time. Horacek led the Cats in scoring, netting eight points.

With the non-conference season complete, K-State took stock of the upcoming Big Six campaign. Iowa State was currently 7-0 and was led in scoring by Gordon Nicholas, who was averaging nine points/game. KU, which had lost the 1940 National Collegiate Title game to Indiana, was expected to be very good, yet was struggling. Jayhawk star Ralph Miller was battling injuries but the Hawks had great scoring from Howard Engleman, who had already netted 87 points in just five games. Missouri was rebuilding and Oklahoma had graduated many key members of its famed "Boy Scats" group. Nebraska, under new Coach Adolph Lewandowski, had the tallest team in the league. The Cornhuskers returned Don Fitz, Sidney Held, Al Randall and Hartmann Goetze. Randall was 6'7" and had proved to be a handful in the non-conference slate. Little was expected from K-State, an underdog role that Coach Gardner was born to play. He promised to have his team ready.

Nebraska (Lincoln): The Cats opened the conference season, losing to Nebraska 33-23. K-State held a slim 13-12 lead at the half, but it was their last lead as the Cornhuskers rallied behind the play of guard Don Fitz to pull away. Fitz scored eight points early in the second half and helped Nebraska to a 21-14 lead. The Cats rallied, led by the scoring of Beaumont, and managed to cut the deficit to just 23-21, but they could not draw any closer as they suffered their sixth straight loss. K-State managed just three of 12 free throws, many missed while the game was still in doubt. Fitz led all scorers with 12 points while Beaumont (nine) and Guy (seven) paced the Wildcats.

Oklahoma (Manhattan): K-State gained their first Big Six victory with a stunning 41-36 overtime triumph over Oklahoma. The Sooners were riding an incredible wave as they entered Manhattan. Just three days earlier, they had defeated KU in Norman. They no doubt had little fear of the "other" Kansas entry in the conference. It was these very situations in which Jack Gardner thrived.

The Cats opened the game blazing, and held leads of three to nine points the entire first half. They settled for a 21-15 lead at the intermission as the K-State faithful prayed that the team had another half in them. In the final period, the Sooners rallied, and finally gained their first lead, 31-30, very late in the contest. The teams traded baskets before OU grabbed a 36-34 lead with just seconds remaining. The Sooners also had the ball but Norris Holstrom stole a pass and quickly found Chris Langvardt down the court. The two-sport star hit the bucket just as the horn sounded, sending the game into overtime and Nichols Gymnasium into an absolute frenzy. In the extra frame, the Cats held OU scoreless while Holstrom and Beaumont tallied for the victory. K-State managed to shoot a paltry 22.2% (14 of 63) from the floor but were 13 of 17 (76.4%) from the charity stripe. Horacek led the Cats in scoring with 12 points as K-State was now tied for second in the conference race.

Nichols Gym again was awash in banners and signs but the students went one step further. Just two days later (January 13), over 1,500 students and the college band staged a noisy parade in both Aggieville and downtown Manhattan. Signs and banners were everywhere, urging the state legislators (who were beginning their legislative session the next day) to fund a new field house. One sign, noting that only students could attend games, read "Haven't Seen a Game in the Cracker Box Since 1920." The campaign to build a new field house was approaching a fever pitch. State legislators and Kansas Governor Payne Ritner were invited to attend the KU game, which was in just a few short days. Although Gardner concentrated on basketball, he seldom passed up a chance to lobby for a new field house. He knew, however, that nothing would reinforce his statements quite as strongly as an exciting team on the court.

Nebraska (Manhattan): K-State avenged an earlier loss and defeated Nebraska, 35-32. The Cats had a stellar defensive effort and led the entire first half, settling for a 16-12 cushion as they left the floor for intermission. NU regrouped, tied the game at 20-20, and took their first lead, 22-20, on a bucket by Sid Held. It was their last lead as K-State edged away. Howe led the Cats in scoring with nine points. Don Fitz, the NU guard who had given the Cats "fits" in Lincoln, was held to just three points. The win vaulted K-State into a first-place tie in the Big Six, setting up a showdown with the Jayhawks.

Kansas (Manhattan): In a game that featured more sights and sounds than a Ringling Brothers Circus, KU edged the Wildcats 46-41. Basketball was almost secondary to everything else! The police escorted 250 state legislators and Governor Ritner to Manhattan to both view the game and the Nichols' atmosphere first-hand. The gym again was decorated with banners and signs and even a surprise. At halftime, a dummy fell from the rafters and landed strategically near the visiting delegation from Topeka. Two students, dressed as medical interns and carrying a stretcher, raced to the "victim" and to the delight of the students, carried him from the premises. The staged dramatics probably amused the governor but the field house issue was not a laughing matter. Ritner and the legislators had already pledged support for a new gymnasium but noted money constraints were a considerable obstacle to the project. One thing was clear: K-State basketball had lost money in 1940 (reported to be $4,000) and additional seats would erase that figure. With the near-frenzy for tickets by both students and townspeople alike, that was a given.

Oh yes, there was a game played as well. The contest was perhaps one of the most even competitions between the two rivals. KU led throughout but never by more than the final margin. The halftime score was 23-22 in favor of the Jayhawks and they kept the Cats at arm's-length until the final gun. The story of the game was Howard Engleman, who hailed from Arkansas City. The KU star entered the game averaging 19 points/game and despite double-

Enthusiasm abounds as rabid basketball fans find seats on Nichols Gymnasium's ancient rafters. For lack of a place to hang them, rafter-sitters were forced to sit on coats. — Courtesy of Kansas State University Archives.

teams, netted 23 points in the victory. Bob Allen, Phog's son, added 11. Howe led the Cats in scoring with 10 points while Guy and Langvardt added nine points each. The loss dropped K-State into a second-place tie with Oklahoma while KU assumed the top perch (by percentage points) in the conference.

Oklahoma (Norman): The Cats ventured from Manhattan for the first time in three games and continued their road miseries, losing to Oklahoma 46-38. K-State was saddled with an additional problem as they prepared for the Sooners. Student registration for the spring semester was held in Nichols Gym (where else?) and the Cats had to travel to Junction City to practice. The change of plans was disruptive to the team's schedule. OU had major incentives in the game. First, they hoped to avenge their only conference loss (suffered to K-State). Second, they were just percentage points behind KU for the top spot in the conference. If Oklahoma could defeat the Cats, they would climb to the top of the conference ladder. The Sooners struck quickly and jumped to a 17-5 early lead. The Cats rebounded and thanks to the play of Langvardt and Horacek, closed the gap to just 22-17 at the half. OU pushed the lead back to ten points in the second half and was not seriously challenged. Both teams managed 16 field goals but the free throw line again plagued K-State. They managed just six of 18 from the stripe. The Sooners nailed 14 of 20. Horacek paced the Cats in scoring, netting 11 points. A.D. "Ug" Roberts led all scorers with 13 for the Sooners.

Missouri (Manhattan): The Cats tightened their hold on fourth place in the Big Six Conference as they defeated Missouri, 34-24. Both teams were extremely cold in the first half of the game, with the Cats clinging to a 15-13 lead over their feline rivals from Columbia. Despite the deficit, Missouri had to feel quite pleased at the intermission. The Tigers, currently occupying the conference cellar, were hampered by the loss of two key regulars (Arch Watson and Keith Bangert) due to scholastic problems. In addition, Herb Gregg, the Tigers top scorer, had to leave the game late in the first half due to a serious knee injury. Despite all of that, MU had to like their chances to pull the upset. Those hopes were quickly dashed, however, as the Cats turned several errant passes into easy buckets and pulled away in the second half. Beaumont, the lanky sophomore from El Dorado, led the Cats in scoring with 12 points. Langvardt added eight as K-State stood with a 3-3 record in the conference race.

Iowa State (Manhattan): In their last home game of the season, K-State lost to Iowa State, 50-41. The game was fast-paced in the first half with 11 lead changes before the Cats closed the half with a flourish and led 32-25 at the intermission. In the second half, K-State could not find the nets and managed just nine points. The Cyclones, however, were in peak form and combined nifty passing with shooting accuracy to claim the victory and move into fourth place in the conference. The loss dropped K-State into fifth place and with three conference games ahead (all on the road), the prospects looked dim for a top finish. Horacek led the Cats with 11 points while Howe added nine. Albert Budolfson (13), Dale DeKoster (11) and Gordon Nicholas (10) paced the Cyclones.

Missouri (Columbia): K-State struggled and lost to Missouri, 30-28. The game started slowly as neither team could muster much offense. By halftime, the teams were tied 12-12. In the second half, the Tigers began to assume control, and with less than four minutes remaining, held a 27-22 lead. Now for some dramatics! Langvardt and Guy each netted a field goal and the Cats clawed to within one point, 27-26. After several missed opportunities by both teams, Norris Holstrom fouled MU guard Martin Nash with less than 10 seconds to play. Nash made the first charity but missed the second, and in the rebounding scramble, Missouri fouled K-State's Dan Howe. The Cat junior from Stockdale calmly hit both charities to tie the game with just five seconds to play. Overtime seemed a certainty, something K-State gladly would accept. Missouri wasted no time, however. A half-court pass found the Tigers' Roy Storm who quickly turned and fired a shot from center court. It found nothing but net as the horn sounded! It was the Tigers' first conference win and a huge disappointment for the Purple, who had entered the game as the clear favorite. Horacek led all scorers with nine points as K-State's conference mark fell to 3-5.

Kansas (Lawrence): K-State pushed the conference-leading Jayhawks to the edge but was defeated in overtime, 50-45 in Lawrence. The Cats opened an early 4-1 lead to the absolute horror of 3,500 loyal KU fans, but the Hawks recovered and led 21-14 at the half. K-State quickly countered, and led by the shooting of Langvardt, Beaumont and Howe, forged a 26-26 tie with 13 minutes to play. From this point until the end, the teams traded baskets in some dramatic play engineered by two of the conference's best coaches, Phog Allen and Jack Gardner. The Cats finally claimed a 41-39 lead before a Howard Engleman bucket with just 20 seconds remaining was the final scoring of regulation. In overtime, key baskets by Bob Allen, Engleman and Vance Hall proved to be the difference as KU won their sixth conference game in seven starts. The victory was also the Hawks' 26th consecutive home triumph. K-State saw its record fall to 3-6 in the conference. Engleman led KU in scoring with 15 points while Allen added 10. Beaumont paced the Cats with 11 points with Horacek chipping in 10.

Iowa State (Ames): The Cats closed out the '41 season with a 36-33 loss to the Cyclones in Ames. Although the game was tight, K-State enjoyed just two leads, both in the first half. Iowa State had the halftime edge, 21-16, and seemed in control until Chris Langvardt went on a late scoring binge. The Wildcat senior scored several buckets in a row, the last forcing a 33-33 deadlock with just two minutes to play. The Cyclones had the final answers, however, and edged away to victory. Langvardt closed out his basketball career by nailing 13 points to lead the Wildcats. Horacek added nine as K-State closed out the season with a 6-12 overall record. The conference title was shared by KU and Iowa State (both ended with a 7-3 mark), with the Cyclones advancing to the playoffs. They would lose to Creighton in their first playoff game. Kansas State ended the conference season with a 3-7 record and a fifth-place finish. Chris Langvardt was named to the second team all-conference squad while Jack Horacek, Tony Guy and Larry Beaumont were honorable mention selections.

K-State continued to press the field house issue and in March of '41, a new proposal was made. The Wildcat hierarchy, working with 4-H clubs across Kansas, asked the state to fund and build a $400,000 4-H Field House that would not only support K-State athletics and the physical education needs of the college, but also would serve as the key facility for the state's nearly 24,000 4-H members. This idea had first been proposed in 1940, but now the state 4-H leadership and its members were totally behind the project. K-State President F. D. Farrell noted that currently Nichols Gymnasium housed athletics, the student radio station, the military science department, literary society rooms, music studios and the public speaking department. The 4-H idea had merit and seemed to be gaining momentum. A certain surprise attack in Hawaii just nine short months later changed the priorities, not only at K-State, but across the nation as well.

Team Statistics (Newspaper box scores):

K-State:	611 points	33.9/game
Opponents:	660 points	36.7/game

Individual Scoring Leaders (newspaper box scores):

Jack Horacek (Topeka, Ks.)	140 points	7.8/game
Tony Guy (Coffeyville, Ks.)	100 points	5.6/game
Dan Howe (Stockdale, Ks.)	90 points	5.0/game
Larry Beaumont (El Dorado, Ks.)	85 points	4.7/game
Chris Langvardt (Alta Vista, Ks.)	81 points	5.4/game
Norris Holstrom (Topeka, Ks.)	50 points	3.3/game
George Mendenhall (Belleville, Ks.)	25 points	1.7/game
Dean Lill (Mt. Hope, Ks.)	21 points	1.3/game
Others	19 points	

NCAA CHAMPION: Wisconsin (20-3)
RUNNER-UP: Washington State
THIRD PLACE: Pittsburgh & Arkansas

1942
A Change of Address

Record: 8-10
Conference Record: 3-7 (5th)

Team Captain: Dan Howe

| Larry Beaumont | Bruce Holman | George Mendenhall | John St. John | Fred Kohl |

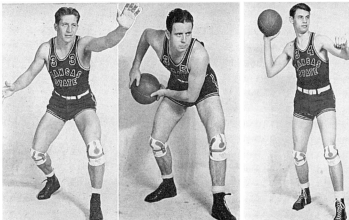

Jack Horacek

| John Bortka | Kenneth Messner | Marlo Dirks | Danny Howe |

— Courtesy of Kansas State University Archives

Jack Gardner opened the 1942 season with some major questions to answer. The Cats did return four lettermen in Jack Horacek, Dan Howe, Larry Beaumont and George Mendenhall. It was a talented group with Horacek the leading returning scorer. The senior from Topeka had averaged 7.8 points/game in 1941, and with Beaumont was an Honorable Mention Big Six selection in the '41 campaign. There were anxious moments about Horacek, however. Just days before returning to school, the Topeka senior broke his leg playing softball. He would be in a cast for six weeks but by all accounts would be ready to play by November. Gardner hoped the four experienced players would lead a very strong group of sophomores, including Bruce Holman, Marlo Dirks, John Bortka and John St. John. This Wildcat team was by far the most athletic that Gardner had fielded but it also was the smallest. Lack of height would be a great concern as the '42 team took on an ambitious schedule. In addition to the conference foes, K-State had two games scheduled against an experienced Colorado State crew. The Cats also would embark on a Western road trip involving Washington, Washington State, Montana and Montana State. Each figured to test every Wildcat muscle.

As the season was set to begin, basketball fans had both eyes squarely focused on Norman, Oklahoma. Gerald Tucker, the Winfield native, was the most heralded sophomore to enter the league in years. Gardner had publicly stated that Tucker was "a once in a decade caliber player," and early practice reports indicated "Titanic Tuck" was all of that and more. Tucker's transfer from K-State in the fall of 1940 had raised a few eyebrows but it was nothing like what would soon transpire. Sports writers would have a season full of stories when the Tucker issue hit the fan!

Doane College (Manhattan): K-State began the season with a 57-43 victory over Doane College. The Cats led throughout the first half and hit the halftime break up 27-17. Doane did manage a brief run in the second period and drew to within four points but got no closer as Horacek (11) and Howe (10) scored in double figures. K-State was a disappointing 11 of 23 from the foul line, and the overall performance by the Purple was less than impressive. There were plenty of issues for the team to work on in the coming practices, but all paled in comparison with the news just three days later: Pearl Harbor! The ensuing war would send many colleges scrambling as young men were drafted and both young men and women left school for war-related jobs and support services.

Colorado State (Manhattan): The Cats won their second game in as many starts, defeating Colorado State 30-25. The game was the first between the two schools since the 1939-40 season. K-State managed a 12-11 lead at the half but took control in the second period to forge a 26-17 lead late in the contest. Back charged the visitors, who cut the advantage to just one point late in the game. The Cats responded, particularly John St. John. The sophomore guard from Wichita netted two quick buckets to stop the rally and preserve the victory for the Wildcats. Horacek led K-State in scoring with 17 points while St. John scored four, the critical four-points late in the game.

Colorado State (Manhattan): The two teams met again just two nights later and the results were the same as K-State edged Colorado State, 37-35. The contest was the tightest ever between the two as neither team could manage more than a four-point bulge. Tied at 35-35, the Cats had the final answer as Horacek nailed a bucket with just two seconds remaining to snare the victory. He led all scorers with 15 points while St. John added eight. Colorado State, led by Owen Smith and Harold Wood (each netting eight points), continued on their sunflower travels with a game at Emporia State before they returned to Ft. Collins.

Washburn (Manhattan): K-State kept their record unblemished as they pounded Washburn, 48-29. Washburn jumped to a 5-0 lead before the Cats found the nets, but when they finally did they ended the suspense. The Wildcats went on a seven-point run and finally knotted the score at 9-9. It was the last tie as Kansas State raced to a 20-12 lead at the half. Washburn had no answers in the second half as the Cats remained perfect with a 4-0 record. Horacek led all scorers with 15 points while Larry Beaumont, a junior guard from El Dorado, added nine.

After the game, K-State immediately boarded the train for a 4,322 mile road trip that would take them to games against Washington and Washington State, followed by stops in Montana and Montana State. The Missouri Tigers would join the Cats for games against both Washington and Washington State. Ten players, Coach Gardner and Assistant Coach O.L. "Chilli" Cochrane would make the trip with the team returning to Manhattan on Christmas Day. The Cats would travel in comfort, however, as Pullman "sleeper cars" were to be their accommodations.

Washington (Seattle): The Cats began the road trip with a disappointing 45-32 loss to the University of Washington. K-State trailed 21-17 at halftime, but then feel prey to a tough Huskies defense and poor execution in the second half. Washington shot an amazing 92 attempts in the game, netting 19 (20.6%). Huskies guard Bobby Lindh poured in 17 tallies for the victors while Horacek added nine for the Cats. It was a rather poor effort by K-State and Gardner wondered out loud if the players may have been a bit "too comfortable" on the trip. He would quickly get to test that theory!

Washington State (Seattle): K-State lost their second straight, this time to Washington State, 47-22. It was an even poorer effort for the Cats, but Washington State was expected to be very good in 1942. The boys from Pullman were the 1941 Western Regional Champions and runner-up to Wisconsin in the national tournament. K-State played a good first half, trailing only 19-16 at the break. They never seemed to return from the intermission, however, as the Cougars totally dominated. For the game, the Cats shot a dismal 15.5% from the field (nine of 58) while Washington State managed 22.8 % (21 of 92). Marlo Dirks, a sophomore from Moundridge, led the Cats efforts with just five points.

The Purple received more disappointment after the game. Those comfortable Pullman "sleeper cars" were gone! The military had a much more urgent need for them, and off they went. The remainder of the trip to Montana and then home would be "roughing it."

Montana (Missoula): K-State played much better and defeated Montana, 44-34. The Cats led 20-16 at the half, and after the Grizzles cut that deficit to just one (20-19) Horacek and Fred Kohl slipped in four straight field goals to push the lead to 28-19. Montana did not recover. K-State had excellent scoring balance as George Mendenhall led the Cats with nine points, while John Borkta added seven. Horacek, Dan Howe and Bruce Holman each added six tallies.

Montana State (Bozeman): The road trip ended in disappointment as the Cats were defeated by Montana State, 45-38. K-State last tied the game at 9-9 before the Bobcats edged away for the victory. Dirks led the Cats in scoring with nine points while Bortka, the sophomore forward from Kansas City, Missouri, added seven. Bortka was the lone Cat who remained from Gardner's 1940 "Dream Team" of recruits. He would figure quite prominently in the '42 season. So would another of those prize recruits: Gerald Tucker, who now was starring at Oklahoma!

As the conference season was set to begin, Tucker was the man, both on and off the court. He quickly had displayed his considerable scoring talents for the Sooners in the non-conference slate. Questions about his transfer from K-State to Oklahoma, however, became the burning issue. Although no formal announcement was made as to who lodged the official complaint, newspapers were not shy in reporting that the grievance was filed by Phog Allen. The KU coach pressed the Sooners and the Big Six Faculty Representatives for some answers.

Big Six rules stated that a school with a "migrant" player must first obtain, from the previous conference school attended, written permission for the player to compete in conference games with his new team. In their deliberations, the faculty representatives ruled that Tucker was indeed a "migrant" player. This case marked the first time since the Big Six was formed (1929) that the "migrant" athletic rule had ever been applied. The Sooners questioned the "migrant" tag being applied to Tucker but they knew they were in a spot. Oklahoma had not obtained the necessary permission from Kansas State. The situation seemed quite clear, yet the faculty representatives, whose responsibility was to enforce the rules, hesitated. Instead of simply ruling Tucker ineligible until both the necessary paperwork and waiting period were satisfied, the representatives turned to K-State to save some face. It was not Kansas State's responsibility to make sure Tucker was free and clear. It was Oklahoma's, yet the conference pushed the Tucker matter back to Manhattan. Conversations between Norman and Manhattan were both fast and furious as the two schools rushed to complete the proper transfer. Phog Allen and the media watched the proceedings closely. Kansas State literally held Tucker's future in their hands. If they refused to release him officially, the young star could see his college basketball days end before they began. Most newspapers agreed, however. Oklahoma got a major break in the dispute when the faculty representatives turned the case over to "the fairest and most honorable man in the entire league," K-State Athletic Director Mike Ahearn. All agreed that Ahearn would treat both Tucker and Oklahoma with absolute professionalism, and he did, agreeing to release the star player from any Kansas State commitments. It was now up to the conference to rule when Tucker could begin to play.

Newspapers around the Sunflower State were not shy. They had little praise for the conference faculty representatives (who seemed more intent in letting Ahearn handle their chores) and felt Oklahoma was trying to "bully" the conference by circumventing normal eligibility requirements.

1942 — A Change of Address

The Sooners had never been shy about asserting themselves in the conference, but this time they hit a brick wall. After all of the paper work was in order, the conference (suddenly with new-found courage) declared Tucker ineligible until the second semester (which would begin in late January). Tucker would miss the first five games of the conference season, including two games against K-State and one against KU. Oklahoma was not pleased with the decision but abided by it. Tucker would sit and wait. When he finally hit the floor, he would hit it with a vengeance.

Nebraska (Lincoln): The Cats opened the Big Six Conference with a 44-38 defeat at the hands of Nebraska. The Cornhuskers dominated the first half and led 21-11 at halftime. That lead grew to 32-13 before K-State made a charge, cutting the deficit to just four points. Nebraska stalled the final minutes to get the win. Bruce Holman, a forward from Powhattan, paced the Cats in scoring with eight points. Horacek chipped in seven. Nebraska was led in scoring by all-conference selection Sid Held, who nailed 13 points.

Oklahoma (Norman): After all the commotion, K-State and Oklahoma met in Norman and the Sooners defeated the Cats, 47-40. Gerald Tucker was in attendance, seated in the balcony, and watched his teammates Paul Heap, Richard Reich and A. D. "Ug" Roberts pour in 37 points for the Sooners. The trio was too much to stop as Oklahoma led throughout and had a commanding 27-19 lead at the half. Dan Howe led K-State with 12 points while Beaumont added eight. The play of Howe was very encouraging. The senior center from Stockdale had struggled earlier in the season with injuries but appeared to find his game in Norman.

If there was any bad blood between K-State and Oklahoma, it did not appear in the game. Both teams played hard and fair. Just days earlier, the reception OU received in Lawrence was quite a different story. At a KU pep rally before the game, Phog Allen reignited the flames when he accused Oklahoma of subsidizing the Tucker move from Manhattan to Norman. The KU coach received a surprise, however, when OU coach Bruce Drake and the Sooner team appeared in the auditorium! Drake asked to speak at the rally and immediately attempted to set the record straight. According to Drake, Tucker was not induced to transfer to Oklahoma and in fact had been "held" in Manhattan for one week before his mother came to take him away. Once Drake had the floor, he was not about to give it up and when Phog Allen passed a note to the Sooner coach informing him that the pep rally had run beyond its allotted time, Drake ignored him. The KU students in attendance loved his every word and encouraged the OU mentor to continue his speech: they were missing class time and were in no hurry to get back! Later that night, without Tucker, the Sooners were pounded by KU, 54-32. Charlie Black, the gifted Jayhawk sophomore, poured in 25 points to lead the effort.

As K-State prepared for a second contest with the Sooners, it was very hard for students across the campus to ignore the war. Newspapers were filled with daily accounts of the Allied efforts and upperclassmen at K-State were naturally quite anxious, certain that they would soon be drafted into the service. The conflict took on a very personal nature, however, on January 13. On that day, Kansas State announced that it had officially received word of the first K-State graduate to die in the war. Lt. Milton Kaslow, class of 1940, was killed on December 31 in action in the Far East. Kaslow was a very active student while on the Manhattan campus and had graduated with a degree in chemical engineering. He was perhaps best known for his involvement in both music and theatrics and had roles in several productions in Manhattan. His death was followed by more grim news. Captain Alvin W. Hamilton, class of 1927, was also killed just days later while serving in the Corregidor Islands. These announcements would be made with painful regularity at Kansas State and at other schools across the country.

Wildcat center Danny Howe stretches to get the tip from an Oklahoma opponent. Bruce Holman (No. 27) and Jack Horacek await results. Kansas State lost to the Sooners, 26 to 25, in the last minute of the game.
— Courtesy of Kansas State University Archives

Oklahoma (Manhattan): In a quick turnaround game, the Cats lost to OU, 26-25. K-State, fueled by their fans, opened the game at a furious pace. The Cats managed a five-point lead at the half (14-9), holding the visitors scoreless for nine minutes. In the second half, OU awoke, and both teams played a racehorse game. K-State enjoyed a five-point spread (22-17) late in the contest when the Sooners made their last run. Oklahoma clamped the defensive pressure on the Cats and pulled ahead, 26-23, with less than three minutes to play. Holman nailed a long bucket to cut the lead to one but Dan Howe's attempt at the buzzer hung on the rim before falling harmlessly to the floor. Statisticians were sent scrambling after the game. The two teams had combined for 125 field goal attempts! It was one thing to take shots. Making them was quite another story. K-State shot 14.7% (10 of 69) while Oklahoma was not much better, blistering the nets with 16.1% shooting (nine of 56). The Sooners managed enough free throws to gain the victory. Bortka led K-State with seven points while Richard Reich led OU with eight. "Ug" Roberts, who tormented the Purple in Norman, was held scoreless by the Cat's George Mendenhall. Gardner, ever the motivator, had reverted to some psychology to inspire Mendenhall. Earlier in the week, the coach had publicly commented that Roberts was the only player that Mendenhall, the junior from Belleville, could not handle. Mendenhall got the message and delivered.

Kansas (Lawrence): K-State again did everything to win the game but lost to KU in overtime, 46-44. As in the past, the stakes were high for both teams. The Cats desperately wanted to end their streak of futility against KU while the Hawks were trying to climb back into the conference race. Gardner, for his part, closed all practice sessions and was quiet around the media.

The Hawks trailed for most of the first half but exited the floor at halftime only down by one, 24-23. Twice KU had to rally in the closing seconds to tie the game and finally knotted the score, 42-42, sending the contest into overtime. In the extra session, KU's John Buescher nailed the final bucket to give KU their ninth consecutive win over their rivals to the west. Horacek led all scorers with 14 points while Jayhawk forward Ralph Miller nailed 12 for the Crimson and Blue.

Nebraska (Manhattan): After numerous close losses, the law of averages finally helped the Cats as they grabbed their first Big Six win, defeating Nebraska 38-35. K-State, playing without Mendenhall (hospitalized with the flu), jumped to an early lead and led 21-15 at the half. The Cornhuskers, who went five minutes in the first half without a bucket, wasted little time in the final period and quickly knotted the game at 25-25. From that point, the contest was tight, but a basket by Howe with less than five minutes to play gave the Wildcats a lead they would not relinquish. Neither team burned the nets: K-State shot 21.7% from the field (15 of 69) while Nebraska hit 30.7% (16 of 52). Charity tosses decided the game: the Cornhuskers struggled at the foul line (just three of nine) while K-State was a respectable 8 of 14. Howe led the Cats with 11 tallies.

Iowa State (Manhattan): Close losses continued to torment K-State as they lost to Iowa State, 44-43. This loss was perhaps the unkindest of them all. The Cats trailed 26-23 at halftime, but quickly rebounded in the final period and seemed to be in control. The Cyclones, however, had one last run and they made their move late in the game. Led by guard Al Budolfson, Iowa State chipped away at the Cats margin and finally tied the game, 43-43, with just seconds to play. Kansas State then committed the unpardonable sin. They fouled the Cyclones' George Harville, and with less than 15 seconds left, the Iowa State guard nailed the winning free throw. The late rally spoiled a splendid effort by Horacek, who led all scorers with 18 points.

Missouri (Columbia): K-State's fortunes continued to decline as they lost to Missouri, 44-36. The Tigers jumped to a 13-0 lead and for all practical purposes had the game won from that point. The Cats played Mizzou on even terms from there, but the damage was already done. Don Harvey led all scorers with 17 points for the Tigers while Bortka managed 11 for K-State. Missouri climbed out of the conference basement with the win while the loss dropped the Cats into sole possession of last place. They would not remain alone in that position for long.

Missouri (Manhattan): The two teams met for the second time in a week and K-State used a late rally to gain their second conference victory as they edged Missouri, 42-35. Paced by good outside shooting, the Tigers jumped to a 18-15 lead at the half. The shooting fortunes changed in the second half and K-State nailed just enough baskets down the stretch to get the win. Marlo

Dirks, the substitute center for the Cats, had a fine game and scored 12 points. Holman added nine for the Wildcats. With the victory, Missouri and K-State now shared the conference cellar, both with identical records of 2-6.

The Big Six spotlight shifted to Norman and the battle between KU and OU. Gerald Tucker was eligible, ready and leading the Big Six in scoring, averaging 17.3 points/game. In an effort to ensure sportsmanship (and perhaps Phog Allen's very skin), the Oklahoma athletic office positioned 100 members of the "O" club in strategic spots around the gym. They were hardly needed as the Sooners got their revenge on the court, defeating the Jayhawks, 63-51. Tucker was magnificent. The former Winfield High star scored 22 points. The win assured Oklahoma of at least a tie for the conference championship. KU was still in the hunt, but had considerable work to do. A date in Manhattan with the Cats would very probably help to decide the Hawks' fate.

Iowa State (Ames): In a considerable upset, K-State edged Iowa State, 36-34. The Purple led throughout thanks to the fine play of Larry Beaumont. The Cat center poured in 14 points, all in the first half, to stake the Wildcats to a 20-19 edge. Beaumont fouled out early in the second half but Howe, Horacek and Holman provided just enough punch to get the win. The victory pulled the Cats out of the conference cellar, which they had shared with Missouri.

Kansas (Manhattan): In their worst effort of the year, K-State pulled down the blinds on the '42 season by losing to KU, 45-26. Both teams started the game with little scoring, but KU began to find the range late in the first half and fashioned a 21-12 lead at the break. As the second-half deficit grew, K-State's shooting woes worsened and they limped weakly into the off-season. The Cats concluded the game shooting just 12.6% (nine of 71) and was eight of 19 (42.1%) from the line. Howe led K-State in scoring with nine points while Ralph Miller led KU with a hard-earned 13 points. The game was not without great K-State effort. Larry Beaumont played outstanding defense on Miller, holding him to just three field goals (in 18 attempts). Beaumont was rewarded for the fine play: he left late in the game with a fractured nose! His injury provided a fitting conclusion to the disappointing Wildcat season. Larry Beaumont, Jack Horacek, Bruce Holman, Dan Howe and George Mendenhall were Honorable Mention Big Six selections. KU and OU shared the conference title with identical 8-2 records. In 1942, ties in the conference were settled by comparing points scored against points allowed (offense-defense ratio). Because the Jayhawks had a better points ratio, they advanced to the national tournament, losing to Colorado in the first round of the Western Regional.

Although one could not necessarily see results in the win-loss column, Jack Gardner had captured the hearts of K-Staters everywhere. In three short seasons, the young coach had made basketball an event on campus, with students and townspeople scrambling for tickets to get into Nichols Gymnasium. Kansas State was also attracting better players each year and the sky was the limit for the program.

That all changed on May 7, 1942. Gardner disclosed that he was leaving K-State to enlist into the Naval Air Training Program. The war was in some of its most intense early days and good men were needed from every corner of the country. The young coach was proud and enthusiastic about his new endeavor. "I consider it a privilege to join the Naval Air Physical

Training Program," said Gardner. "I plan to do my part to train young naval pilots to become the strongest and toughest fighters the world has ever seen. I leave Manhattan with great sadness but look forward to returning to Kansas State after the war." Gardner left for Annapolis, where he would receive his training from the physical education department of the Navy. He had some familiar company: C.S. "Cooney" Moll, K-State's swim coach for the past 13 years, joined him in the same program.

Athletic Director Mike Ahearn publicly voiced his support of Gardner and hoped that once the war ended, the young coach would return to the Flint Hills to guide the Cats. In the interim, Ahearn appointed O. L. "Chilli" Cochrane to be the new Kansas State coach. Cochrane, a star quarterback for the Cats from 1924-26, had assisted Gardner and knew the basketball program well.

Team Statistics (Newspaper box scores):

Kansas State	676 points	37.6/game
Opponents:	703 points	39.1game

Individual Scoring Leaders (Newspaper box scores):

Jack Horacek (Topeka, Ks.)	117 points	6.5/game
Bruce Holman (Powhattan, Ks.)	105 points	5.8/game
Larry Beaumont (El Dorado, Ks.)	103 points	6.1/game
Dan Howe (Stockdale, Ks.)	92 points	5.1/game
Marlo Dirks (Moundridge, Ks.)	59 points	3.7/game
John Bortka (Kansas City, Mo.)	50 points	4.4/game
John St. John (Wichita, Ks.)	43 points	2.7/game
George Mendenhall (Belleville, Ks.)	38 points	2.7/game
Fred Kohl (Kansas City, Mo.)	36 points	2.6/game
Ken Messner (Arkansas City, Ks.)	28 points	1.9/game
Others	5 points	

NCAA CHAMPION: Stanford (28-4)
RUNNER-UP: Dartmouth
THIRD PLACE: Colorado & Kentucky

1947

Talent in the Flint Hills

Record: 14-10
Conference Record: 3-7 (tie for 5th)

Team Captain: Bruce Holman

Kansas State Basketball Squad, back row: Jack Gardner, Marlo Dirks, Jerry Patrick, Dave Weatherby, Rick Harman, Fritz Knorr. Front row: Lloyd Krone, Al Langton, Bruce Holman, Joe Thornton, Keith Thomas, Harold Howey, John Dean.
— Courtesy of Kansas State University Archives

It's Time To Play

In the four years that Jack Gardner was gone from Kansas State, Wildcat fans had few chances to cheer. During that time, three coaches (Chilli Cochrane, Cliff Rock and Fritz Knorr) led the Cats onto the hardwoods with very little success. In conference play, the best the Wildcat's could muster was a fifth-place finish in 1945 with a record of 4-6. Overall, the team had a four-year record of just 27-62 (8-32 in the conference). K-State fans endured losses to such teams as Washburn, Rockhurst, Norman (Oklahoma) Naval Air Station, Fort Riley, Great Bend Air Force Base, Herington Air Force Base and the Olathe Naval Air Station. The Olathe losses were of particular interest: coaching the Olathe team was none other than Jack Gardner himself! There also were 11 straight losses to KU, the worst being a 25-point Jayhawk rout in 1946. This was the second widest margin of victory for the Hawks in the series, only surpassed by a 26-point pounding in 1935. All told, it was a rather dark time to be a Kansas State basketball fan.

The war years had been a confusing time to follow college basketball. It was a good bet that many fans had to continually check their programs! Rosters were in a state of constant flux as players came and went due to the military draft. Some players returned as decorated war heroes while others gave the ultimate sacrifice and never returned from their service in the European and Asian theaters. Kansas State struggled with this roster uncertainty but the Cats were not without some talented players. Both Jay Payton (Emporia) and David Weatherby (Neodesha) were All-Big Six performers in the 1945 and 1946 seasons. Weatherby also shared the Kansas State single-game scoring record (28 points against Iowa State) with former Wildcat All-American Frank Groves (1937). Payton would graduate in 1946 but Weatherby would return for the 1947 season. For Wildcat fans, there were two key questions to be answered about the '47 campaign: who would coach the team and who would the coach recruit?

The answer to the first question was an exciting one. Jack Gardner was back in Manhattan, still brimming with the confidence and energy of his days before the war. Gardner had spent much of World War II as an athletic director for the Navy Aeronautic V-5 Pre-flight School. The V-5 Program was a comprehensive training regiment that, in simplest terms, helped train men for war through sports. In addition to specific pilot training, instruction was also emphasized in many sports. Each sport provided its own specific skill that would assist the young man in military service. Basketball, for instance, taught hand and eye coordination and trained for instant and correct decisions. Track taught speed and timing while boxing taught self-assurance, courage and aggressiveness in battle. Football, gymnastics, cross country, wrestling and soccer also were emphasized. Teams were formed from various squadrons and competed against each other. Competition was intense and the aim of each contest was to develop "ruthless determined competitors." The sporting competition was very physical, and many times the rules were relaxed to allow for even more contact. Each contest was designed to show the cadet that there was no substitute for winning. "Gracious defeat" should be forgotten! In addition to his athletic director position, Gardner also supervised the building of many physical training facilities around the country. He also found time to coach basketball at both the Olathe Naval Air Station and at military facilities around San Diego. The V-5 program was dismantled in June, 1946, but not until nearly 80,000 cadets and 2,500 instructors participated in the training.

After a four-year wartime absence, while serving as a naval officer, Jack Gardner, head basketball coach, returned to Kansas State to tutor the 1946-47 cage team to one of the best records in school history.
— Courtesy of Kansas State University Archives

With Jack back in Manhattan, the second question had an even more exciting answer. Gardner would work with the finest talent ever assembled in the Flint Hills. During the war years enrollments fell as men were called into military service. With smaller numbers in school, freshmen were ruled immediately eligible for varsity play. With the war just completed, the yearlings would remain eligible and Gardner had lassoed some dandies in freshmen Rick Harman (an All-Stater from Hosington), Clarence Brannum (a native of Winfield) and Allan Langton from Eureka. In addition, Gardner added Keith Thomas (an All-State performer from Wyandotte High who had played for Gardner at the Olathe Naval Air Station), John Dean, a sophomore from Harveyville (who had played on the Memphis Hellcats basketball squad, the third-ranked service team in the country) and sophomore Harold Howey, a former star at Iola Junior College who also played for Gardner at the Olathe Naval Base. Another key player would be Lloyd Krone, who played at the University of Oklahoma and also at Washburn University, where he attended the V-12 military training program. Weatherby would bring all-conference experience to the group. With Gardner and a collection of talent unmatched in memory, K-Staters could hardly wait for the arrival of the round ball season of 1947.

Ft. Hays (Manhattan): On December 2, 1946, in an unusual occurrence, K-State opened the season with two games on the same night. In the first game, the Cats had a real struggle but edged Ft. Hays, 48-40. The Tigers took the early lead and pushed K-State the entire game, trailing by just two, 24-22, at the half. Early in the second half, Hays took their last lead, 26-24, before the Wildcats edged away for the victory. Erv Bussart and Lloyd Krone led the Cats in scoring with nine points each while Bob Blazer and Herb Settles led Ft. Hays with 11 points apiece.

Washburn (Manhattan): In the second contest of the evening, K-State had a much easier time as they whipped Washburn, 47-27. Washburn also jumped to an early lead until the Cats tied the game, 6-6. There would be no further ties as K-State pulled away to a halftime lead of 21-11. In the second half, the lead ballooned as John Dean sparked the Cats. Dean led all scorers with 12 points while K-State's Harold Howey added nine. Tom Carlson paced Washburn with 11 tallies. K-State prepared for their first road trip with games scheduled against both Drake and the University of Iowa. Gardner had used the doubleheader against Washburn and Ft. Hays wisely. A total of 18 players had seen action. From that group, Gardner and Assistant Coach Dan Howe chose 14 to make the trip into Iowa.

Drake (Des Moines): In a double-overtime thriller, K-State grabbed a 46-43 victory over Drake. The Cats came out strong and jumped to a 17-11 lead at the half. It had the makings of a cakewalk until Drake's John Pritchard stopped the music. In the second half, Pritchard scored 13 points and helped pull Drake to a 26-22 lead. K-State fought back and had a one-point advantage when Pritchard nailed a free throw to send the game into overtime. Fortunately for the Cats, he would not score again.

In the first overtime, K-State twice had three-point leads only to see Drake battle back. The first extra period ended with the teams tied, 41-41. In the second overtime, John Dean finally settled the issue in favor of K-State. Dean nailed a long field goal with less than 30 seconds left to give the Cats a 45-43 lead. After a Drake miss, Dean was fouled and added the final point to end the dramatic evening. Dean led the Cats in scoring, netting 12 points, while David Weatherby added 11. Pritchard ended the game with 14 points, 13 scored in the second half.

Iowa (Iowa City): The Iowa Hawkeyes captured their 22nd consecutive home victory over a non-conference foe as they defeated the Cats, 54-41. The Purple held a comfortable lead throughout most of the first half, but a late Iowa rush gave the home team a 26-21 lead at the intermission. K-State drew no closer as Iowa used a basket barrage to pull away. Noble Jorgensen led all scorers, netting 16 points for Iowa. Dean and Jerry Patrick led K-State, nailing seven points each.

As the Cats returned to Manhattan, they had to prepare for something new. Beginning in the 1943-44 season, both KU and K-State had participated in a four-team, invitational holiday tournament in Kansas City. This tournament would evolve and the 1947 season would match all six conference teams for the first time. Entering the tournament, the conference had a combined record of 13-1 (K-State's loss to Iowa was the only blemish). This holiday bash would give the fans a chance to size-up their team and the other conference foes. Joining the six members were two invited guests from the Southwestern Conference, SMU and Arkansas. Both were considered favorites. The Cats traveled by car to Kansas City but before they left Gardner named Keith Thomas, the former All-State guard from Wyandotte High, to be the team's captain in the first-round battle with Oklahoma. K-State entered the game as a 20-point underdog, a role that never intimidated Gardner!

Oklahoma (Kansas City): In a stunning upset, the Cats defeated Oklahoma, 59-55. The Sooners led for nearly the entire game until K-State finally crawled even, 41-41, with six minutes remaining. They never looked back and steadily pulled away to victory. Oklahoma was paced by "Titanic Tuck," Gerald Tucker. Tucker had returned from military service and was still the dominating player Gardner knew he would be (only wearing the wrong-colored uniform). Tucker poured in 24 points but he could not offset the Wildcat balance as Howey (16) and Dean (14) paced the Cats. KU, SMU and Arkansas also grabbed first-round wins.

Southern Methodist (Kansas City): The invited SMU Mustangs advanced to the finals of the Big Six Tournament as they defeated Kansas State, 46-36. A crowd of more than 5,000 fans watched the much taller Mustangs dominate the Cats for most of the game. K-State, down 31-18 at halftime, did manage a nice run late in the game but drew no closer than three points. John Dean was the only Cat in double figures, netting 11 points. Buro Rollings, the SMU guard, poured in 13 to lead the Mustangs.

Arkansas (Kansas City): In another stunning victory, K-State upset Arkansas, 56-41, to claim third place in the holiday tournament. The Cats used their best defensive effort of the year, holding the Razorbacks to just three field goals in the first half. Up 34-19 at the intermission, K-State coasted to the victory. David Weatherby paced the Purple in scoring, netting 15 points. Howey added 14. SMU claimed the tournament title by defeating KU in the championship tilt.

Drake (Manhattan): Kansas State returned from the holiday tournament with renewed confidence and pounded Drake, 74-37. The Cats held a slim 29-21 lead at the break, then responded with an offensive output not seen in recent years. The 74 points were the most scored by a Wildcat team since Kansas State tallied 70 against Nebraska in the 1945 season. Earlier, it seemed Drake would make it a game. The Bulldogs tied the game at 21-21 before K-State scored the next 17 points to take control. Weatherby led the Cats in scoring with 13 points, while Rick Harman added 10. Marlo Dirks and Dean chipped in nine apiece as the Cats displayed the most offensive balance of the year.

Wichita (Wichita): Kansas State handed Wichita University its first loss of the season as the Cats defeated the Shockers, 48-41. Before more than 4,000 fans in the Wichita Forum, K-State took an early lead and never relinquished it. The Purple enjoyed a six-point lead at halftime, quickly stretched it to 10 points early in the second half, and then withstood one last gasp by Wichita to notch their seventh win in nine starts. Dean nailed 10 points to lead the scoring for K-State.

Montana State (Manhattan): It was a rare event for K-State fans on December 28, 1946. The Cats defeated Montana State, 51-40. The victory was not rare. The townspeople attending the game were! During the war years, the enrollment at K-State had dropped and townspeople were allowed to purchase limited tickets to some games. Once the war ended, the enrollment increased and the games again became the sole dominion of the students. The demand for tickets by "outsiders" continued to grow, however, and since the students were on their Christmas break, K-State decided to make tickets available to the general public. They were quickly gobbled up.

Montana State was quite good. Their stop in Manhattan was the last game of an East Coast tour. The Bobcats were led by Ray Kuka, a guard who had starred at Notre Dame before transferring to Bozeman. He was a handful (scoring 16 points) and personally kept the Bobcats close until the last four minutes of play. Up by only two points, Weatherby and Dean scored key buckets to give the Cats some breathing space, and finally the win. Dean paced the Wildcats with 14 points.

Washburn (Topeka): In one of the tightest struggles ever, K-State nipped Washburn, 42-40, on a David Weatherby basket with just 45 seconds remaining. It was the second Cat victory over the Ichabods in the season, but in no way, shape or form did it resemble the easy 47-27 win to start the '47 campaign. Washburn, except for two early ties in the game, led throughout. The Ichabods held a four-point bulge (21-17) at the half and continued to keep K-State at arm's length for most of the second period as well. Washburn managed its largest lead, 39-33, with less than four minutes to play. The Wildcats, led by Harman, Howey and Dirks, managed to cut that lead to one, 40-39, before a foul shot by Dean knotted the game at 40-40. Washburn lost possession of the ball, and with 45 seconds left Weatherby nailed a long bucket for the lead. The Ichabods had one more chance but missed a free throw opportunity and K-State grabbed the victory. Harman led K-State's scoring with nine points while Morley Fraser led the Washburn attack with 10 points. With the conference season just around the bend, the Wildcats improved their record to 9-2.

Nebraska (Manhattan): Kansas State began the conference slate in fine fashion as they defeated Nebraska, 63-54. The game revolved around one player: K-State's Harold Howey. The forward from Kansas City, Missouri, poured in a career-high 27 points in a dominating performance. His total was just one point shy of the school's single-game record (28 points), shared by David Weatherby and Frank Groves. The Cats needed every point! The game was tight throughout with 18 lead changes and numerous ties. The Cornhuskers held a slim 29-28 lead at the half (Howey had 14 at the break) and enjoyed their largest lead, 46-42, with less than 12 minutes to play. The Wildcats dominated from that point as Howey, Harman, Dean and Clarence Brannum provided the firepower to get the win. In addition to Howey's career night, David Weatherby also was in double figures with 10 points. Nebraska was led by Claude Retherford (18) and Joe Brown (16).

Iowa State (Ames): In an improbable upset, Iowa State snapped K-State's six-game winning streak and defeated the Cats, 51-40. The Cyclones entered the game having lost nine straight contests, and after one half it appeared Kansas State was set to deliver on number 10. The Wildcats led 26-19 at the intermission, but in the second half struggled in every aspect imaginable. The Cyclones made quick work of the K-State lead, tied the game at 30-30, and were off to the races. Howey paced the Cats with 11 points while Keith Thomas added eight. Jim Myers and Don Paulsen led the Cyclones with 13 points each.

Missouri (Manhattan): In an overtime loss, Kansas State was defeated by Missouri, 43-42. The game was close throughout, with the teams knotted at 16-16 at halftime. In the second half, the Tigers maintained a slight advantage, and were up 36-32 with less than two minutes to play. The Cats rallied and tied the game at 36, sending the contest into overtime. In the extra session, Missouri's Darrell Lorrance hit two free throws and a field goal to help decide the contest. The foul line hurt the Purple. They had numerous chances at the charity stripe but managed to hit just 14 of 25 from the line. Howey paced the Cats, netting 11 points while Thomas added nine. The Tigers' Dan Pippin, an all-conference selection, led all scorers with 17.

Oklahoma (Manhattan): The pot had been simmering for several years and it finally reached the boiling point as Oklahoma pounded K-State, 50-30, in a fight-filled contest. The Sooners, anxious to avenge the upset loss to the Cats in the holiday tournament, jumped to an early lead and never let up in sending K-State to their third straight defeat.

Oklahoma started quickly and by halftime led 17-12. As the second half began, the Sooners went on a 18-3 run to promptly end any drama, or so they thought. That is when the real fireworks began! K-State center Jerry Patrick and OU guard Allie Paine became entangled on a rebound, and as they were separated, began swinging at each other. Gerald Tucker, the OU star who had contributed to Kansas State's nightmares both on and off the court, joined the fray. Both Patrick and Paine were tossed, and as Patrick walked past the OU bench, he and Tucker decided to enter into round two. Neither connected with anything resembling a punch, but just two minutes later, the Sooners' Charlie Pugsley and the Cats' Norm Rothrock began to mix it up. Rothrock, a Cat footballer, connected several times (one paper termed them "resounding blows") and the two were first separated and then thrown from the game. Tucker led all scorers with 19 points while Howey led K-State with nine.

Rockhurst (Manhattan): On January 20, 1947, the Cats ventured out of conference and defeated Rockhurst, 51-44, to stop their three-game losing streak. In the first half, the contest was close as neither team could command more than a four-point lead. K-State led 28-25 at the half, and after a brief 31-31 tie in the second period, gradually pulled away to snare the non-conference victory. Howey led the Cats in scoring, tossing in 15 points. All told, 10 Wildcats found the scoring column in the contest.

This game has become very important in Kansas State Basketball history. The win was K-State's sixth home victory of the season, guaranteeing the Cats a winning record at home. Beginning with the 1947 season (and to the present date), Kansas State has never known a losing record at home. As of 2007, the streak is now at 61 seasons, an NCAA record! It all began rather quietly on a cold night in January, 1947.

One streak was painfully known. The Purple had lost 21 straight to KU, who was the Cats' next opponent. As K-State prepared for the Hawks, injuries were beginning to multiply in Manhattan. John Dean, K-State's most consistent player all season, injured his hand during practice and would see limited action. Keith Thomas, the Cats' best defender, was struggling with a knee injury while Norm Rothrock, the Wildcat footballer who had begun to show real promise at guard (just ask OU's Charlie Pugsley), had to quit the squad indefinitely due to back problems brought on from football. All three players were guards, a position that now would be manned by Allan Langton, native of Eureka, and former Winfield star Joe Thornton, who had played well on the Cats' "B" squad.

KU had some problems of their own, namely coaching. Phog Allen was sidelined with some recurring health problems caused when he sustained a nasty fall in practice earlier in the season. Howard Engleman, the former KU star who was Allen's assistant, now assumed the reins. The Hawks had plenty of talent, however, led by Charlie Black, Ray Evans, Harold England, Owen Peck and Otto Schnellbacher. With that talented crew, KU had more than enough punch to extend the streak!

Kansas (Lawrence): KU extended their personal win streak over Kansas State to 22 games as they plastered the Cats, 50-39. The Jayhawks, with the exception of the first several minutes of the game, were in complete control in a contest that also saw some tempers reaching the boiling point. The Cats tied the game at 4-4 before KU took off, scoring the next six points on the way to a 30-20 halftime bulge. K-State trimmed the deficit to six points but got no closer. Black (13), led a balanced KU attack that saw nine Jayhawks score. Dean and Thomas paced K-State with seven points each. Yes, these two were "walking wounded" prior to the game, yet both saw extensive action. Was Gardner up to some trickery? If so, KU clearly was not fooled by the injury report.

The game was not without controversy. The official scorers tallied the final score as 50-39, but the newspaper tally sheets indicated the score should have been 50-40. Gardner caught the error early in the second half. K-State trailed 35-26, but it actually was 35-27 as the scorers failed to register a John Dean free throw. Gardner protested but lost the argument and the game. In the end, the controversy meant little, except perhaps to Dean. With the win, KU climbed into a tie with Nebraska for fourth in the conference. K-State plunged deeper into the conference cellar. Phog or no Phog, K-State was still "in the fog" when it concerned KU!

Iowa State (Manhattan): The Cats claimed their second Big Six victory as they defeated Iowa State, 43-30. With the win, the two teams were now deadlocked for fifth place in the conference standings. The game was perhaps the most ragged of the season. Both teams were careless with the ball and a combined 53 fouls were whistled (26 on the Cats). The fouls may have been even, but the results were not. K-State nailed a commendable 19 of 31 charities while Iowa State hit 14 of 28. Those foul shots, many early in the second half, helped the Purple expand a 20-16 halftime lead into a 13-point advantage, which is how the game ended. A total of 11 Cats scored, led by Howey's nine points.

The Wildcats did make some news off the court. The team unofficially adopted Gary Thomas, the two-year-old son of Keith Thomas, as their basketball mascot. The younger Thomas admired all the Cats, but felt his dad and Dorrance, Kansas, forward Ken Mahoney were simply the two best players in the world. Neither would argue with the young fan's assessment.

Missouri (Columbia): K-State played it close for all but five minutes, but those minutes were crucial as the Cats lost to Missouri, 49-43. The two teams battled evenly until the Tigers edged ahead in the final five minutes to secure the victory. With the win, Missouri stood 5-1 in the conference and assumed sole possession of first place. Thornton Jenkins led MU with 13 points while Harold Howey netted 10 for the Cats. Coach Gardner was personally involved in a critical moment in the game. The Wildcat boss was assessed a technical foul. In the first half, Gardner protested a foul called on Keith Thomas. The K-State guard was whistled for the infraction as the Tigers' John Rudolph made a long field goal. Gardner rushed onto the court and expressed his displeasure with the officials. A technical was called and Rudolph made both free throws (one for the Thomas foul and one for the technical) resulting in a four-point possession for the Tigers. Although the incident was early in the contest, it proved costly in the end for the Cats.

Oklahoma (Norman): K-State was no match for the Sooners, losing 57-38. Oklahoma again jumped to an early lead, stretched it to a 23-18 bulge at the half, and then drove away in a cloud of red dust in the second period. Gerald Tucker, in his last game against K-State, was his usual dynamic self, scoring 18 points at the center position. Dick Reich added 13 for the Sooners. Howey led K-State with eight points. The victory (and a Missouri loss to Iowa State) pushed Oklahoma into first place in the Big Six. The Cats' conference record fell to 2-6. The prospects for many more wins looked bleak: next-up was a rematch with KU.

The 22 game losing streak to the Jayhawks was on everyone's mind. KU needed another win to keep pace in the conference race. K-State needed the win to put the prolonged nightmare finally to rest. If the Hawks could win, the streak would have eclipsed 10 full seasons! Tickets, always the rarest of gems for K-State basketball, became even rarer for this game. Because Nichols Gymnasium officially seated only 2,800 fans, this particular game would be open only to students who possessed maroon-colored activity books. Students began lining-up in the halls of the athletic office early in the week to hopefully receive the coveted book. Green-and-maroon colored books were handed out alternately and several fist fights erupted amongst the fans as they jockeyed for favorable position in the line! Frank Meyers, the Wildcat business manager, had to close the ticket office during one day because of the behavior of rabid fans. Tickets were just one element of the upcoming game. As game day approached, the Cats were saddened by one bit of news. Marlo Dirks, the Wildcat center from Moundridge, had to return to his home town due to the death of his small child.

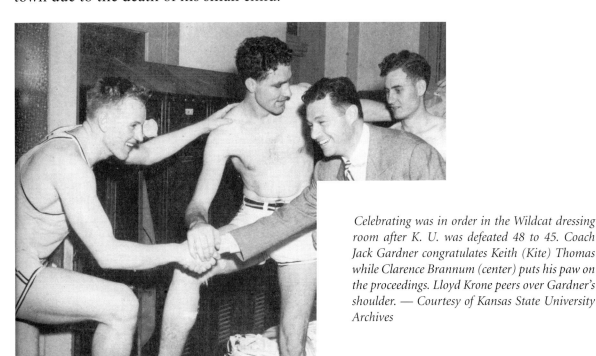

Celebrating was in order in the Wildcat dressing room after K. U. was defeated 48 to 45. Coach Jack Gardner congratulates Keith (Kite) Thomas while Clarence Brannum (center) puts his paw on the proceedings. Lloyd Krone peers over Gardner's shoulder. — Courtesy of Kansas State University Archives

Kansas (Manhattan): The long streak was over! Kansas State finally defeated KU, 48-45, in a thrilling game that had more than its share of drama and fouls. The officials whistled 63 fouls in the contest (33 on KU) as seven players were sent to the bench with disqualifications. KU saw four leave the game: Otto Schnellbacher, Owen Peck, Charlie Black and Ray Evans. K-State lost three players because of fouls: Clarence Brannum, David Weatherby and Harold Howey.

The streak initially seemed safe as the Jayhawks opened a 8-0 lead early in the game. K-State fans were already beginning to mutter: Why had they fought so hard (literally) to get these tickets? The Cats recovered, however, and led by Thomas, Brannum, Weatherby and Dean, managed to tie the game (21-21) at the half.

The second half was a seesaw battle, but fouls were starting to pile up on the Hawks. Schnellbacher left the game just two minutes into the second half, and Peck and Black would soon follow. Coach Howard Engleman, still leading the Jayhawks in Coach Allen's absence, was forced to substitute early in the final frame. With Howey and Thomas carrying the load, K-State finally broke free and grabbed a 45-36 lead as the fans began to anticipate the win. Not so fast! Back roared the KU starters (what was left of them), led by star guard Ray Evans. The Hawk great personally commanded the charge that cut the Cat lead to just 46-44. K-State had the answer, however, and finally ended the "Jayhawk Jinx." College officials also rejoiced in the win. They proclaimed a school holiday for the next day. Time for that much-awaited celebration. No doubt, Aggieville would serve as "the place to be!"

The play of Keith Thomas was a huge factor in the Cats' win. Thomas netted 16 points and played some stellar, frustrating defense in the process. Dean (nine) and Weatherby (eight) also provided offensive support. Marlo Dirks did return for the game, managing one point. KU was paced by Charlie Black, who flipped in 12 tallies. The Jayhawk star did miss six free throws, however, many in the first half when the Cats were on their heels. The loss sent the Hawks into fourth place in the conference and eliminated any chance of them winning the title.

Wichita (Manhattan): K-State made it two wins in a row, defeating Wichita 60-41. It was the Wildcats' 11th non-conference victory in 13 chances. The Shockers managed an early lead, perhaps in part to the KU hangover, but Gardner finally got the Purple into gear and they led 26-22 at the half. The visitors drew no closer as Clarence Brannum paced the Cats with 13 points, his best game of the year. Brannum, just a freshmen from Winfield, was the twin brother of Bob Brannum, a basketball star at the University of Kentucky. The K-State Brannum had shown great defensive prowess for the Cats, but now was starting to find some offense as well. Harman also netted double figures, flipping in 10 points. Wichita's Jim Nebergall led all scorers with 17.

Nebraska (Lincoln): The Cats lost to Nebraska, 54-50, to close out the conference portion of the season. K-State trailed much of the first half but stayed within one (31-30) at the intermission. The Wildcats quickly broke from the gate in the second period and at one time led, 42-37. They could not sustain the momentum and the Cornhuskers edged into the lead and finally the win. The loss ruined a tremendous performance from the Cats' Howey, who led all scorers with 23 points. Bob Cerv paced Nebraska with 13. With the defeat, K-State fell into a fifth-place tie with Nebraska, as both ended the conference season with records of 3-7. Oklahoma captured the conference crown with a record of 8-2. It was the Sooners' first undisputed title since 1929. Oklahoma advanced to the national championship game only to lose to Holy Cross, a team that featured Bob Cousy. He would figure quite prominently in the K-State picture in 1948!

Bradley (Peoria): K-State ended the '47 season with a 48-41 loss to Bradley. The Cats stayed close for only one half of the first period before Bradley began to pull away. Down 24-18 at the half, K-State was unable to ever gain the lead. Patrick and Howey paced the scoring with nine points each.

The Wildcats closed out the 1947 campaign with a 14-10 record, their most wins in a single season since 1931. That year, Kansas State posted a 11-6 mark under the direction of Coach Charles Corsaut. Several Wildcats received post-season honors. Howey was selected to the All Conference Second Team, while Dean received honorable mention accolades.

One other bit of significant news occurred as the conference season wound down. On March 1, 1947, the Big Six added a new member: Colorado. The 19-year reign of the Big Six was officially over. One team clearly dominated the now-defunct conference: Kansas. The Jayhawks and Phog Allen had won or shared 12 basketball titles. KU's closest competition was Oklahoma, which won or tied for six titles. As for K-State-- well, the Cats won zero titles. The Big Six had not been kind to the Purple. Much better days were ahead in the Big Seven!

Team Statistics (Newspaper box scores):

Kansas State:	1131 points	47.1/game
Opponents:	1080 points	45.0/game

Individual Scoring Leaders (Newspaper box scores):

Harold Howey (Kansas City , Mo.)	222 points	10.1/game
John Dean (Harveyville, Ks.)	163 points	7.4/game
David Weatherby (Neodesha, Ks.)	122 points	5.3/game
Keith Thomas (Kansas City, Ks.)	102 points	5.1/game
Rick Harman (Hoisington, Ks.)	99 points	4.3/game
Lloyd Krone (Chanute, Ks.)	88 points	3.7/game
Marlo Dirks (Moundridge, Ks.)	85 points	3.9/game
Clarence Brannum (Winfield, Ks.)	81 points	3.7/game
Jerry Patrick (San Diego, Cal.)	68 points	3.0/game
Bruce Holman (Powhattan, Ks.)	33 points	1.5/game
Allan Langton (Eureka, Ks.)	21 points	1.2/game
Erv Bussart (Wamego, Ks)	11 points	1.8/game
George Mann (Canton, Ohio)	11 points	1.0/game
Others:	25 points	

NCAA CHAMPION: Holy Cross (27-3)
RUNNER-UP: Oklahoma
THIRD PLACE: Texas
FOURTH PLACE: City College of NY (CCNY)

1948

On the Big Stage

Record: 22-6
Conference Record: 9-3 (1st)

Team Captain: Howard Shannon

Back Row (left to right): Assistant coach Tex Winter, Jack Bell, Dave Weatherby, Clarence Brannum, Ward Clark, Jerry Patrick, Rick Harman, head coach Jack Gardner. Middle Row (left to right): John Dean, Harold Howey, Al Langton, Lloyd Krone, Bob Lewis, Howard Shannon. Front Row (left to right): Bill Aye, Ken Mahoney, Joe Thornton, Bob Johnson, Bill Thurston, trainer John Trubacek. — Courtesy of Kansas State University Archives

As the 1948 basketball campaign approached, there was not a lot of "love" for the K-State squad. The Cats returned significant talent from the 1947 team, but that group had placed fifth in the final year of the Big Six. It was not clear if Harold Howey, Rick Harman, Jerry Patrick, John Dean, Allan Langton, Ken Mahoney, David Weatherby and Clarence Brannum had improved to a level that would help the Cats ascend the conference rankings. One other factor blurred the picture. The Big Six was now the Big Seven and Colorado figured to be quite good. With all of these variables to consider, most experts had K-State destined for a nice, quiet fourth or fifth place finish. The prognosticators missed the mark on two accounts. First, all of the above basketball players WERE better, significantly better. Second, the Cats had always seemed to lack that one player who would help put them over the top. In the fall of 1947, K-State found that player. His name was Howard Shannon.

Shannon, from Munday, Texas, had already played considerable college basketball prior to arriving in Manhattan. The Texas guard had stops in a Texas junior college and a Texas Teachers college before Jack Gardner spotted him playing for the Continental Airlines AAU team. Gardner convinced Shannon that Manhattan was where he should continue his war-interrupted education. The '47 Cats relied on speed whenever possible. It proved to be a decisive edge for them. With Shannon, the Cats got faster and that edge became sharper.

There was one significant rule change that would affect the 1948 season. Beginning on September 1, 1947, the Big Seven Conference reinstated the one-year residency rule. The rule, suspended during the war years, required that an athlete must first spend one year in residence at a conference school before he could become eligible to participate in varsity sports. Gardner had signed a heralded group of freshmen in the spring of '47 (Ernie Barrett of Wellington was one of the gems) but these yearlings would have to show their wares on the junior varsity during the '48 campaign.

Rockhurst (Manhattan): The Cats opened the season with a convincing 52-37 victory over Rockhurst. The Hawks from Kansas City grabbed an early lead but K-State wrestled control of the game midway through the first half. The Purple led 25-18 at the half and then outscored Rockhurst 17-4 in a second half blitz to grab the win. Rick Harman led the scoring efforts, pouring in 16 points while Harold Howey added 13. Paul Martel paced Rockhurst with 10 points.

Culver-Stockton (Manhattan): In a relatively easy game, K-State pounded Culver-Stockton (Canton, Missouri), 55-34. The Cats jumped to a 27-19 lead at the half as Howey scored 11 points in the first stanza. K-State kept up the pressure in the second half and at one time hit Culver with a 12-0 scoring spurt. That outburst pushed the Cat lead to 20 (46-26) and Gardner cleared the bench. One of the reserves, Ken Mahoney of Dorrance, had perhaps the most "artful" play of the night. Late in the contest, Mahoney took a pass at the free throw line and bounced the ball back through his legs to a driving Howey, who was cutting to the basket. Howey hit the lay-up while the crowd went wild with the "no look" completion from Mahoney. Howey ended the game with 15 points while Howard Shannon added 13. Culver was led by 6'7" Lew Hitch, who scored 10 points. Gardner was quite impressed with the big center and the feeling must have been mutual: Hitch would transfer to Manhattan and become a Wildcat in 1949.

Texas Christian University (Manhattan): In a dazzling performance, K-State smashed TCU 75-17. The Wildcat fast break was in race mode as the Cats jumped to a 41-6 lead at the half. It only got worse for the Horned Frogs, who never recovered. K-State's tight defense limited TCU to few shots, and even those were of poor quality. Nine Wildcats scored, led by 15 points from Shannon. Dean (14) and Howey (13) also found double figures. The game was a near-record performance for the Purple. The 75 points were the second most ever scored by a Kansas State team, only surpassed by the 76 points scored against Kansas Wesleyan on March 3, 1911!

In the early schedule, the Cat's fast-paced offense was a thing of beauty, but Gardner was hardly married to the style. The Cat boss was more than anything else, a pragmatic coach. Although he preferred a faster tempo, Gardner played whatever style best suited his players, and speed certainly suited this bunch. "With high-strung kids like Harman, Howey, Langton, Shannon and the others, I have to play a race horse style of ball," said Gardner. "Speed is second nature to these boys." This high-powered offense, coupled with a smothering defense, was a proven recipe for championships. Although it was early in the season, it appeared K-State possessed all of the necessary ingredients to far exceed those predictions of another dismal finish in the conference.

Indiana (Kansas City): The Cats kept their record unblemished as they defeated Indiana 61-53 in a game played in Kansas City. The Hoosiers enjoyed just one lead (2-0) before Harman, Dean and Howey began an offensive assault. With just six minutes gone from the game, the Cats led 15-5 and they nursed that lead until the final horn. K-State had great balance: Howey led the Cats with 11 points while Shannon and Ward Clark added nine points each. Harman and Dean also had good games, each netting eight points apiece.

K-State remained in Kansas City and prepared for the Big Seven Holiday Tournament. The eight-team field was completed when the Oklahoma A&M Aggies (today's Oklahoma State) were invited to play. The Aggies, a dominating member of the Missouri Valley Conference, were engaged in a courtship of the Big Seven. A&M wanted to join the conference and the Big Seven had some interest as well. At a December, 1947, faculty representative meeting, the possibility of A&M joining the Big Seven was discussed but the notion was tabled for another day. It seemed clear that the Aggies would someday become a new member of the conference. For now, the time did not seem right.

Oklahoma (Kansas City): Before a crowd of more than 2,000 fans, K-State defeated Oklahoma 55-48, in their opening round game in the holiday tournament. The Sooners raced to a 9-3 early advantage before the Cats grabbed their first lead of the game, 14-13. The contest remained tight until the end, but K-State used some timely foul shooting to grab the final margin. Shannon paced the Cats' scoring with nine points while Ken Pryor led OU with 11. KU, Nebraska and Oklahoma A & M also grabbed first-round wins.

Kansas (Kansas City): K-State disposed of KU, 56-42, to gain entrance into the finals of the holiday tourney. The '48 season was expected to be a rebuilding one for KU. Gone were All-Americans Charlie Black and Ray Evans. The two stars had led the Hawks to three conference titles. In addition, the Jayhawks played without standout Otto Schnellbacher, who was in Miami with the KU football team, preparing for a match with Georgia Tech in the Orange Bowl. The KU fortunes had so turned that earlier in the year they were pasted by Emporia, 67-44! This was K-State, however, and Gardner knew the rivals from Lawrence would be ready.

The Cats led the entire first half and enjoyed a 26-18 halftime lead. KU came back strongly, however, and finally tied the game at 29-29. After several lead changes, the Wildcats pulled away to victory, their second straight over the Hawks. Harman and Clark led the Cats in scoring, each netting 10 points. Harold England paced the Hawks with 10 tallies.

Oklahoma A & M (Kansas City): K-State claimed their first holiday tournament title as they defeated the Aggies, 50-43. Before a raucous crowd of 8,500, the Wildcat's speed and aggressiveness were too much for the slower, more methodical visitors. Howey led the Cats' attack, netting 18 points as K-State improved its record to 7-0. A & M suffered its first defeat in seven games.

Ft. Hays (Manhattan): K-State won their eighth straight game as they easily defeated Ft. Hays, 60-32. The Cats opened the game with a 6-0 lead before Hays settled in to play. The Tigers, trailing 22-17 at the half, started the final frame on a 4-0 run and trailed by just one, 22-21, before K-State zoomed away to victory. The Purple shot 32.3% (23 of 71) from the field but held Hays to just 17.1% shooting (12 of 70). Clarence Brannum, the big Wildcat center, led the scoring efforts with 13 points while Shannon added 12. Dick Englesman, the Tigers 6'8" pivot, led Ft. Hays with nine tallies.

K-State settled into a short, two-day Christmas holiday as one of only 30 undefeated teams in the country. That record was about to be tested. The Cats were about to embark on a three-game, Eastern road trip which included games against Canisius, St. Joseph's and Long Island University. Before they left, Gardner took the team to Salina, where they practiced before more than 200 high school coaches who were attending a coaching clinic conducted by Gardner. It was good exposure for the Cats. Because of the quaint size of Nichols Gymnasium, most of the state could only read about the team. Now, more coaches could view the team first-hand. It also gave Gardner a chance to foster relationships with high school coaches, many of whom were coaching future college talent.

Canisius (Buffalo, NY): Kansas State remained perfect, defeating Canisius, 47-45, before 5,485 fans. The game was extremely close throughout with K-State clinging to a 25-24 lead at the half. The second half was no different as the Purple were unable to distance themselves from the Griffins. A Clarence Brannum basket late in the game pushed the Cats to the final margin and the visitors from Manhattan held on for the win. Howey (14) and Brannum (13) paced the Cats' offense while Canisius was led by star Leroy Chollet, who nailed 15 points.

St. Joseph's (Philadelphia): K-State improved its record to 10-0 with a 59-44 victory over St. Joseph's. The Cats maintained a precarious lead throughout the first half and settled for a narrow 25-22 lead at the intermission. In the final period, it was all K-State as they used their speed and quickness to open a much more comfortable margin. Brannum managed 10 points to lead the Cats, while Langton added nine. With the 10-0 start, Kansas State was now just one of 16 major schools which still had an undefeated basketball squad.

Typical of hustling Rick Harman's rebounding work was this action against St. Joseph's.
— Courtesy of Kansas State University Archives

Long Island (New York City): The Kansas State perfect season ended as Long Island University upset the Cats, 65-47, before 18,000 fans in Madison Square Garden. K-State played well in the early going and showed no signs of stage fright before the huge crowd. The Cats led 9-5 before Long Island outscored the Purple 27-13 to grab a 32-22 lead at the half. For much of the second period, the lead stood before the Wildcats finally made their move. Late in the game, the Cats actually took a two-point lead. They faltered down the stretch, however, and LIU pulled away for the win. K-State could not handle the height of Long Island, particularly Jack French and Ed Anderson (both over 6'5" tall). The two grabbed numerous rebounds and poured in 28 points between them. Howey (12) and Shannon (11) led the Cats, who returned home to begin conference play.

Earlier in the season, K-State was projected as the fourth or fifth best team in the conference. Now, they were cast as the favorite. It was a new role for the Wildcat players. It was a role made much more complicated by Phog Allen. The Kansas coach began to privately question the eligibility of K-State's Clarence Brannum. Allen announced that he had written Gardner a letter. In the letter, Allen wondered how Brannum could have withdrawn from school in the spring of

1947, play in two national AAU tournaments in Denver and then return to the K-State campus in September and immediately become eligible for the '48 season. K-State responded with a letter of their own, stating that after a thorough review, Kansas State found no violations and cleared Brannum to play. Allen was not satisfied and went to the media, publicly questioning Brannum's status. Thurlo McCrady, the Kansas State Athletic Director, charged that Allen was resorting to a "cheap publicity" stunt. "It seems to be a tradition with Allen to put blasts in the papers from time to time," said McCrady. "I for one am getting sick and tired of it. Throughout the entire coaching profession, Allen is being laughed at for these publicity methods of his. It is just a case of cheap personal publicity on the part of Allen." The KU skipper was undaunted and continued to press the issue. Clarence Brannum would remain in the news. Phog Allen would guarantee it!

Colorado (Manhattan): K-State opened the conference with an easy 65-51 victory over Colorado. The Buffaloes, a preseason pick to win the new Big Seven title, were never in the game as K-State hit nearly 50% of their field goals and raced to a 37-13 lead at the half. Colorado struggled so badly that they did not make their first field goal until 16 minutes of play had elapsed! Gardner substituted freely in the second half and Colorado managed some commendable play until the final horn. Four Cats found double figures: Harman (13), Howey (12), Shannon (12) and Dean (11). After just two conference games, Colorado's title hopes were already in shambles. Just two days earlier, KU had blasted the Buffs by 13 points. So much for preseason polls.

Iowa State (Manhattan): K-State won its second conference game, defeating Iowa State 61-42. The game was close for the first half, with the Cats holding a slim 24-22 lead at the intermission. The Purple exploded in the second half and in short order had pushed that lead to 20. For the game, the Cats shot 21 of 55 from the floor (38.1%) while Iowa State managed to hit just 19.1% (13 of 68). Brannum led the Cats with 10 points, while Dean, Shannon and Lloyd Krone each added nine. After the game, K-State received some additional good news. The conference officials concurred with the Wildcats: Clarence Brannum was eligible. It appeared the issue was finally settled.

Drake (Manhattan): The Cats kept winning, defeating Drake 56-45 in a non-conference match. The game was an interesting coaching battle. Drake was tutored by Fordy Anderson. The Bulldog mentor had played for Gardner at Modesto, California. The two had battled twice before with Gardner winning both games against his former player. In the first meeting, the Cats edged Drake 46-43 and in a return game, blasted the Bulldogs 74-37. Gardner glowingly proclaimed that Anderson was one of the finest players he had ever coached. In addition, Gardner was certain that the 28-year-old coach was quickly becoming a fine basketball skipper.

The Cats struggled in the first half and managed a slim 23-17 lead at the break. In the second period, K-State edged away from the Bulldogs as John Dean played a stellar game, scoring 15 points. Brannum added 14 as K-State improved its record to 13-1. The contest was the 23rd between the two schools, with K-State owning a 18-5 record.

As Kansas State reveled in some richly-deserved basketball attention, Phog Allen was still not satisfied about Clarence Brannum. Allen announced that, while he did not like protests, he did write other conference coaches about Brannum, urging them to question their athletic directors. Although the conference faculty representatives had recently ruled Brannum eligible, Allen wanted to know just how they arrived at that decision. He hoped more schools would raise the same question, and possibly force the conference to either change the ruling, or at least define the process of decision-making.

Allen was a coach who had little time for detective work but he knew the media and believed they would run with the story. They didn't disappoint! From their research, it appeared that the conference faculty representatives had voted to allow Brannum to play "out of respect" for Dr. H. H. King, the Kansas State Faculty Representative and Chairman of the Big Seven Eligibility Committee. As the story was reported in several news outlets, Brannum concluded the '47 season with the Cats and then withdrew from school to play A.A.U. basketball. Before doing this, however, Brannum first asked Dr. King if it would be possible to return in 1948, provided his classroom grades were sufficient. King reportedly told Brannum he would be immediately eligible, which was contrary to the rules of the conference. Big Six rules had stated that a player who participated during a semester and then withdrew from school prior to the conclusion of that semester was ineligible for one full calendar year. The conference was now the Big Seven, however, and all of the old Big Six Conference rules were being codified and reprinted into the new conference charter. In the transition process, it became apparent that Dr. King made a major mistake in interpreting Brannum's leave of absence. King, now aware of his blunder, explained the whole case in a letter to Sam Shirkey of the University of Missouri. Shirkey was the Secretary of the Big Seven Conference and he in turn circulated the letter to all of the faculty representatives for their vote on Brannum's status. The faculty representatives decided that King's mistake was an honest one. The committee also felt that Brannum had acted in good faith based upon information he both sought and was given. On January 29, by telephone vote, the committee ruled that the Winfield center was eligible. The matter was closed, or so they thought. Allen was hardly pleased with the decision and would have much more to say in the coming weeks!

Nebraska (Lincoln): The Cats kept winning, defeating Nebraska 64-45 before the second largest crowd (8,700 fans) ever to witness a NU game. The Cornhusker fans had little to cheer about. K-State struck early and built a commanding 34-17 lead at the half. They were not threatened as Harman (12) and Shannon (11) paced the winning efforts. Now 3-0 in the conference, K-State remained tied with KU for the top spot. Kansas State also received more acclaim. A national survey listed the Cats as the number three team in the country, just behind New York University and Texas. Gardner took the opportunity to again propose the construction of a new field house, one that would seat 15,000 fans. The media had nicknamed Gardner "Jack the Builder" and slowly "the Builder" and his Wildcats were putting all the necessary stones in place.

Colorado (Boulder): The Wildcats continued a firm hold atop the conference standings with a 50-44 victory over Colorado. K-State led throughout the game and had a 10-point lead in

the second half before the Buffs made a final push. Colorado cut the lead to just a single bucket but key baskets by Brannum and Harman helped the Purple pull away to victory. Brannum led the scoring with 14 points while Harman added 11. Kendall Hills and Bob Rolander (a graduate of McPherson High School) topped Colorado with 13 points each. It was the Buffaloes' fifth straight conference loss.

Mike Ahearn — Courtesy of Kansas State University Archives

K-State was at the pinnacle of success with a record of 15-1 when it received some very bad news. On February 5, Mike Ahearn passed away. Called the "Father of Kansas State Athletics," Ahearn had retired in 1946 after having been ill for several months. Born in Rotherham, England in 1878, Ahearn and his nine brothers and sisters came to the United States in 1882. He attended Massachusetts State College and was a star athlete in football, basketball, baseball and ice hockey. Ahearn graduated from MSC with a degree in horticulture and came to Kansas State and received his Master's degree in horticulture in 1904. The next year, he was named athletic director and coach of all sports, a position he held until 1910. In five seasons as the Cats' basketball mentor, Ahearn's teams won 28 games and lost 27. From 1910-20, Ahearn returned to the horticulture department at Kansas State. In 1920, he was summoned to replace Z.G. Clevenger as the athletic director.

Ahearn continued in that position until 1946. In his time, he helped turn Kansas State from a small college into a prominent member of the Big Six Conference.

Ahearn was widely known and respected around the country as a gentleman first and an opponent second. Former rival R.E. Hanley, who coached against Ahearn, toasted the "Little Irishman" when he said Ahearn was "the most sincere and completely honest man in intercollegiate athletics." It was unfortunate that he did not see two of his crowning achievements: the 1948 team, which was surpassing even the wildest K-State dreams, and a new field house (which would be formally named for Ahearn on February 12, 1955). It was Mike Ahearn who had listened to the advice of USC coach, Sam Barry, in 1939. Barry knew of a great coach K-State should consider: His name was Jack Gardner.

On February 7, funeral services for Ahearn were held at Seven Dolors Catholic Church in Manhattan. Ahearn was later laid to rest in Framington, Massachusetts, his hometown. Dignitaries from around the state and conference coaches and officials paid their final respects. Phog Allen attended, but couldn't seem to resist the opportunity to question the Brannum issue one more time. After the funeral, Allen was asked to comment about the eligibility of the Winfield Wildcat. The KU coach blasted the NCAA and its' feeble enforcement of rules. Allen encouraged the NCAA to appoint a "Judge Landis" type czar who would cure most of the ills in college athletics. If such a czar existed, Allen was quite certain Brannum would not have played a single game for K-State. It had appeared that the Brannum "fire" had burned itself out just a few weeks earlier. With a few well-placed words by Coach Allen, a new spark rekindled the blaze!

Missouri (Columbia): After a perfect 4-0 start in the conference, K-State suffered its first defeat, 48-46, to the Missouri Tigers. The Cats dominated the first ten minutes of the game before MU surged ahead, holding a 25-21 lead at halftime. K-State never regained the lead, although they cut the deficit to just two with less than 30 seconds remaining. The Cats twice intercepted MU passes and had possession of the ball and a chance to tie the game. Both possessions resulted in K-State turnovers. Shannon (13) and Harman (11) led the Cat scoring while the Tigers' Dan Pippin, who was the leading scorer in the conference, lived up to the billing as he torched the nets for 24 points. Missouri kept one streak intact: they had not lost to K-State in Columbia since 1937.

With a week before their next game, the varsity scrimmaged against the freshmen for the second time of the season. The varsity narrowly won, defeating the yearlings 77-73 before a capacity crowd in Nichols. The game was open to the townspeople, who seldom saw even a glimmer of basketball action all year. Those attending got to see the future Wildcats, including Ernie Barrett, a star from Wellington. Barrett led all scorers, tossing in 18 points. Clarence Brannum led the varsity with 15 tallies.

Oklahoma (Manhattan): Sooner forward Paul Courty nailed a 45-foot bomb with just six seconds remaining as the Sooners defeated the Cats, 49-47. K-State had grabbed an early 4-0 lead before Oklahoma responded. The first half saw five ties as the teams battled evenly until the Sooners finally inched ahead at halftime. They never trailed again, although the Cats finally forced a tie, 46-46, with just two minutes remaining. Both teams exchanged free throws and the contest appeared destined for overtime before Courty's bucket. The Sooner star netted 20 points to lead all scorers while Ward Clark led the Cats with 10 points. The loss dropped K-State into second place in the conference race, one game behind Missouri. Next up, a game with the Jayhawks.

As KU and K-State prepared for their upcoming game in Manhattan, tensions between the two schools could not have been higher. With all of the media attention KU had manufactured, the name Clarence Brannum just may have had more recognition across the state than that of Governor Frank Carlson himself! As the game approached, even the governor became immersed in the pre-game frenzy. An anonymous businessman (the *Lawrence Daily Journal World* said he was from Manhattan while the *Topeka Daily Capital* said he was from Lawrence) requested that the governor assign additional police protection for Coach Allen while he and the team were in Manhattan. The letter stated that the Brannum issue was now so intense, Coach Allen was in danger of bodily harm. Governor Carlson publicly acknowledged the request, did not reveal the author's name and made no promise of action. For his part, Coach Allen expressed little anxiety about the upcoming trip. Coach Gardner prepared a letter to the student body, reprinted in the *K-State Collegian*, reminding the students of appropriate conduct. The letter was a few days late to stop several pranks. K-State students gave the Jimmy Green statue on the KU campus a fresh coat of purple paint and included the sign "Down with Phog: Brannum Stays." In Manhattan, the statue of William Alexander Harris also received some new colors more suitable for KU. One street sign in Lawrence read: "Ban Brannum: Yeah, Phog." No more hype was needed: Bring on the game!

It's Time To Play

Kansas (Manhattan): K-State, playing one of their finest efforts of the season, pounded Kansas, 48-29, strengthening their chances at a first-place position in the conference. KU's strategy from the opening tip was clear: slow the game down, and they did quite nicely. With KU in a stall mode, K-State went nearly nine minutes before netting their first points. The Cats took their first lead, 5-3, and led 14-9 at the half. KU attempted just two field goals in the first half (they made both) but opened up the offense in the final frame. When they did, they were simply no match for the speedy Cats, who roared to victory. For the game, KU managed just seven field goals. Harman (13) and Shannon (10) led the efforts for K-State while Jerry Waugh led KU with nine tallies. There was not a hint of any violence from the crowd, which confined its energies to deafening cheers for the Purple. With the loss, KU was all but eliminated from any conference title contention.

Missouri (Manhattan): In a dramatic game, K-State edged Missouri, 55-53, to continue their run toward a conference title. The game had much less anticipation than the KU game, but twice the drama. Missouri led 19-15 at the half as the two teams battled on nearly even terms. The Tigers withstood an early second half Cat run, and with just seven minutes remaining, seemed in control, leading 48-40. Back came K-State, led by Harman, Brannum and Shannon. The three personally guided the Cats, forcing a 51-51 tie with just seconds remaining. Shannon, who netted eight points in the game, hit a long one-hander to give the Purple its first lead since early in the second half. Missouri responded and Pleasant Smith nailed a basket with eight seconds remaining to again tie the contest, 53-53. K-State hurriedly took the ball out-of-bounds and Clarence Brannum swished a half-court bomb as the buzzer sounded to end the game. Harman led all scorers with 17 points while Brannum, the hero, added 13. The victory, squeaky as it was, improved the Cats conference mark to 6-2, while Missouri fell to 5-4.

Iowa State (Ames): In another tight game, K-State edged Iowa State, 54-48, to remain firmly ensconced as the conference leader. The Cats jumped to an early lead but had to settle for a 28-28 tie at halftime. In the second half, the Cyclones began to dominate and held a six-point lead with just eight minutes left on the clock. K-State came to life, led by Shannon, who scored six quick points. His play turned the game and the Cats opened their own six-point bulge, which they held until the end. Brannum (14), Harman (11) and Shannon (10) paced the Cats' scoring. Ray Wehde led all scorers with 15 points for Iowa State.

Nebraska (Manhattan): K-State stretched its conference lead to two-full games with a 56-49 victory over Nebraska. The game had the appearances of anything but a Cat triumph. Nebraska raced to a 18-5 lead and enjoyed its largest lead, 28-11, before the Purple trimmed the lead to 28-18 at the half. As the second half began, there was little hint of a K-State victory. John Dean and Harold Howey were ice cold and found themselves on the bench. Clarence Brannum was in major foul trouble and joined the pair. In their place, David Weatherby, Allan Langton and Ward Clark were inserted and they led the rally. The trio paced the Cats, who finally tied the game at 36-36, and helped propel K-State to the win. The three subs accounted for 28 points, and combined with Harman and Shannon, proved to be a very capable line-up. Harman ended the game with 14 points (13 in the second half) while Weatherby, Shannon and Langton all netted 10 points each. Clark added eight as K-State improved its conference record to 8-2 (19-3 overall).

KU was next, and the game presented K-State with the opportunity to win its first and only conference title in the 20-year history of the Big Six, now Big Seven. There was another streak that played into the contest as well: K-State had last defeated KU in Lawrence on December 14, 1934. That amounted to 14 straight unsuccessful trips to Mt. Oread. The Jayhawks not only wanted to continue the Wildcat misery in Lawrence, but also wanted to avoid a KU rarity: the conference cellar!

Howlingly happy K-Staters rushed Coach Jack Gardner off his feet after the K.U. game played at Lawrence. The one-point victory was the signal for mass demonstrations, a 1:30 a.m. curfew declared by the Dean of Women, and a surging, pushing, clamorous crowd besieging the President and the president of the Student Council for a school holiday. The game cinched the Big Seven basketball crown, besides being a thrilling triumph over the school down the river.
— Courtesy of Kansas State University Archives

Kansas (Lawrence): Clarence Brannum's free throw with just 30 seconds remaining gave K-State a hard-fought 61-60 victory over Kansas. The win gave the Cats their first conference basketball title since 1919 and ended the 14 game losing streak to KU in Lawrence. Early in the game, it had the appearances of just another lopsided KU victory.

For more than 32 minutes of play, the Jayhawks dominated, led by two-sport star Otto Schnellbacher. The Jayhawk from Sublette was at times unstoppable, finishing with 24 points in the game. He helped propel KU to an early lead, which grew to a 16-point advantage at the midpoint of the second half. With eight minutes to play, the Cats began their rally. With several quick scoring bursts, K-State gained the momentum and finally tied the game, 58-58, with three minutes to play. KU regained the lead, 60-58, but Rick Harman netted a bucket to force the final tie before Brannum turned hero (again) and nailed one free throw to gain the win. For the contest, KU shot 35.1% from the floor (19 of 54) while the Cats shot 27.2% (24 of 88). Shannon (14), Brannum (13) and Harman (13) paced the championship Cats. Kansas State officials disappointed the Manhattan campus when they announced after the game that there would be NO school holiday. Gardner's victories over KU were becoming more common. If he kept up the pace, the students would be missing far too much class.

The conference title could not be overstated. K-State had last won a title in the 1919 season as a member of the Missouri Valley Conference. That team, coached by Z.G. Clevenger, posted a 10-2 conference mark (and an overall record of 17-2). The win was also K-State's fourth straight over the Hawks, something not matched since the Cats captured five straight during the 1918-19 seasons. It was also Kansas State's 20th win of the year, a first for the school.

More news materialized after the game. K-State would play Oklahoma A&M (the Missouri Valley Champion with a record of 26-3), with the winner representing the Fifth District in the upcoming Western NCAA Basketball Playoffs. The game would be played in Kansas City. For A&M, this playoff was rather commonplace. The Oklahoma Aggies had won back-to-back NCAA titles in 1945 and 1946 and had represented the Missouri Valley in the playoffs in the 1939, 1940, 1942, 1945 and 1946 seasons. For K-State, it would be a first!

Oklahoma (Norman): Kansas State closed out the conference slate with a 56-52 loss to Oklahoma. The Cats led for most of the first half before a late Sooner rush gave the home team a 30-28 lead at the half. The Wildcats never regained the advantage as OU stars Ken Pryor (20) and Paul Courty (15) scored points from every conceivable angle. K-State was led in scoring by Howie Shannon, who finished with 15 points. Brannum and Harman added 12 each as the Cats closed out the conference with a record of 9-3 (20-4 overall). With the win, Oklahoma concluded the season with some satisfaction. Two of K-State's four losses were suffered at the hands of OU, and Oklahoma A&M, the other Fifth District finalist, also lost to the Sooners.

As the Cats prepared for the playoff, post-season awards began to be announced. Both Howard Shannon and Clarence Brannum were named to the AP First-Team All Conference squad. Rick Harman and Harold Howey were chosen to the All-Conference "honor roll," which had replaced the usual selection of second team players. In addition, the Associated Press announced that it would soon release its first AP All-American Team. K-Staters certainly felt several Wildcats (Shannon, Harman and Brannum) deserved recognition for this team as well.

Clarence Brannum, who had not answered any eligibility questions for several weeks, was about to enter the news once again. On March 1, 1948, the Big Seven Faculty Representatives formally rejected a motion by KU representative Dr. W.W. Davis, to have Brannum declared ineligible for one calendar year beginning on September 1, 1948. The Brannum issue was now officially closed! Gardner was pleased, but blasted "certain people" who continually would not accept earlier conference decisions that were made in January. "I never had any doubts," said Gardner. "I did enjoy watching others in the conference get excited about his eligibility. It just proves a good man can always win against an unjust charge."

Phog Allen decided to weigh in one more time. The KU boss informed the media that he would not be attending the upcoming Kansas State-Oklahoma A&M game, but felt it was a good idea for someone to begin immediately checking on the eligibility of K-State players for next season. "Some of these players have already used up their allotted college playing time," said Allen. He also indicated that he just might write a book about the whole matter. "I am fortunate," concluded the KU coach, "that I have some additional interesting information for a new book!"

Oklahoma A&M (Kansas City): Kansas State defeated Oklahoma A&M, 43-34, to earn the right to represent the NCAA Fifth District in the Western Division Playoffs. The Cats were forced to use a patchwork lineup as both Howey and Brannum played sparingly due to injuries.

Howey had injured a rib in practice earlier in the week while Brannum was having trouble with a bothersome knee. The Cats' fast break was in high gear in the first half, however, as they rolled to a 27-17 lead at the break. In the second half, K-State turned conservative, very conservative. The Cats attempted just six field goals (making two) and were content to spread the floor, holding the ball and taking their chances on the foul line. It worked as K-State converted 12 free throws in the final period and dispatched the favored Aggies to get the win. Shannon and Wendell Clark provided the offensive punch, leading the Cats in scoring with 15 and 11 points respectively. With the win, K-State joined Washington, Baylor and Wyoming in the Western Division Playoffs. The Eastern Division Playoffs consisted of Holy Cross, the defending NCAA champion, Michigan, Kentucky and Columbia.

Kansas State began to prepare for Wyoming, the 1943 NCAA champion. The Cowboys traveled to Kansas City sporting a record of 18-7. The pundits agreed: although Holy Cross returned all of the players from the 1947 championship team (including a certain guard by the name of Bob Cousy), Kentucky was the team to beat. In the west, Baylor or K-State seemed to be favored by most.

Wyoming (Kansas City): Before a capacity crowd of 9,700 fans, Kansas State advanced to the finals of the NCAA Western Division Playoffs with a 58-48 victory over Wyoming. The Cats grabbed an early lead and were not challenged in posting their 22nd win of the season. K-State had great balance as Shannon (14), Dean (12) and Harman (12) all scored in double figures. In the other game, Baylor edged Washington, 64-62, to also advance to the finals.

Baylor (Kansas City): The Baylor Bears staged a second-half comeback and edged K-State, 60-52, to advance to the national championship game against Kentucky in New York City. The Purple played a solid first half and led 32-28 at the intermission. It took Baylor just three minutes in the final half to draw even with the Cats, and the teams traded baskets until just six minutes remained. Tied at 49-49, Baylor pulled ahead and then spread the floor, converting easy buckets as the Cats chased them over the court. Harman and Shannon led the scoring with 12 points each while Howey added 11. K-State also would travel to New York City to play Holy Cross for the third-place trophy.

Holy Cross (New York City): In the third-place game, Holy Cross defeated K-State, 60-54, ending the Cats' dream season with a record of 22-6. For most of the first half, it appeared the Wildcats had left their game in Kansas City. The Crusaders jumped out quickly and at one time had a 16-point lead. Shannon, who scored 10 points in the first stanza, managed to keep K-State in proximity, and the teams hit the intermission with Holy Cross up 36-24. Kansas State awoke in the second half as Harman, Howey and Dean made quick baskets. Suddenly, there was a game! The Cats proceeded to hit the Crusaders with a 16-4 punch and the game was tied, 40-40, with 11 minutes to play. That was as close as K-State got as Holy Cross went on their own 8-2 run to cement the victory. Shannon was clearly the star. The guard from Texas nailed 17 points and outplayed the Crusaders' Bob Cousy (who managed just five points). Dean (12) and Howey (10) also hit double figures. The Cats shot just 56% from the foul line (14 of 25) and many of the missed chances proved quite costly in the end. Kentucky captured the NCAA title by defeating Baylor in the championship game.

With the season complete, the Associated Press announced its All-American squads. Howey, Brannum and Shannon all were honorable mention selections. In addition, the Helms Foundation named Shannon a First Team All-American. Shannon was also rated as the third-best free throw shooter in the country at 87.9% (58 of 66). In the process, the Texas Wildcat established a new national record by having made 33 consecutive charities. This was also a conference record, surpassing the 15 consecutive free throws made by Oklahoma's Gerald Tucker. Shannon's mark would be a Kansas State record until Steve Henson made 48 in a row in the 1987-88 season.

The 1948 Kansas State team is firmly fixed in K-State history. The squad not only established that K-State would be a challenger each and every year for conference titles, but also launched the Cats on a national stage as well. The excitement created by the team, coupled with the dream of Mike Ahearn, was steam rolling Kansas State toward a new field house. No more nibbling around the edges: Kansas State had arrived as a major basketball program and with 11 lettermen returning, the 1949 season promised to be an even better year. How differently things would look at the end of the summer!

Team Statistics (Newspaper box scores):

K-State:	1539 points	55.0/game
Opponents:	1281 points	45.8/game

Individual Scoring Leaders (Newspaper box scores):

Howard Shannon (Munday, Texas)	276 points	9.9/game
Rick Harman (Hoisington, Ks.)	262 points	9.4/game
Harold Howey (Kansas City, Mo.)	245 points	8.8/game
Clarence Brannum (Winfield, Ks.)	229 points	8.2/game
John Dean (Harveyville, Ks.)	172 points	6.1/game
Ward Clark (Eureka, Ks.)	120 points	4.3/game
Allan Langton (Eureka, Ks.)	98 points	3.5/game
Lloyd Krone (Chanute, Ks.)	61 points	2.2/game
David Weatherby (Neodesha, Ks.)	34 points	1.6/game
Ken Mahoney (Dorrance, Ks.)	21 points	1.3/game
Others	21 points	

NCAA CHAMPION: Kentucky (36-3)
RUNNER-UP: Baylor
THIRD PLACE: Holy Cross
FOURTH PLACE: Kansas State

1949

A Spadeful of Dirt

Record: 13-11
Conference Record: 8-4 (3rd)

Team Captains: Lloyd Krone & John Dean

The 1949 Kansas State Basketball Team - Back row: Ed Head, Ernie Barrett, Rick Harman, Clarence Brannum, Bill Dresser, Jack Stone. Second row: Fred Winters, freshman coach and varsity scout, Henry Specht, Joe Thornton, Lloyd Krone, John Dean, Ken Mahoney, Jack Gardner, head coach. Front row: Al Langton, Bob Johnson, Dan Upson, Norman Mortimer, Don Button, John Trubacek, trainer. — Courtesy of Kansas State University Archives

When we last left Jack Gardner, the Kansas State coach had to be sitting on top of the world. His 1948 team had won the school's first conference title in nearly 30 years and had also played in the Final Four. All five starters were returning (plus six additional lettermen) and several heralded sophomores (including Wellington's Ernie Barrett) would be joining the mix. Gardner's only worry seemed to be choosing who would make the traveling squad. The 1949 team looked to be a real challenger not only for another conference title, but also for national honors as well. How quickly things can unravel!

In May of '48, the Big Seven Conference reversed course and declared Howard Shannon ineligible for the 1949 season. Before enrolling at K-State, Shannon had played two seasons at a Texas junior college (North Texas Agricultural Junior College) and one season at North Texas State Teachers College. Under previous Big Six rules, two years of junior college play had translated into one-year of lost eligibility at a four-year school. By a vote of 5-2, the Big Seven Conference changed the rule. Both K-State and KU voted against the rule change (several KU football players would also be affected). Kansas State agreed in principle with the new rule, but felt it was not fair to punish current players who had made college decisions based upon the previous rule interpretation. The conference turned a deaf ear to an appeal: Shannon was done at K-State. One down, two to go!

A second bombshell hit the Cat program. Although he had one year of eligibility remaining, Harold Howey decided to graduate in the summer of 1948. Howey had accomplished a lifelong dream: playing in the NCAA playoffs. The victories over Oklahoma A&M and Wyoming would always be a cherished memory for the Cat star. Scratch another starter from the list.

Gardner's last hopes of a relaxing summer ended with a third piece of news: Clarence Brannum withdrew from school. Brannum, who had survived a full-court press from Phog Allen, was feeling a financial pinch and left Manhattan for employment opportunities. The Cats, who just weeks earlier looked as strong as any team in the country, now had just two returning starters (Rick Harman and John Dean). Gardner had plenty of questions to answer as the 1949 season began.

Emporia State (Emporia): The Cats opened the season with a decisive 60-49 victory over Emporia State. K-State unveiled three sophomore starters (Ernie Barrett, Ed Head and Jack Stone) along with juniors Rick Harman and Allan Langton. All played significant roles with Harman leading the early charge. After six minutes of play, Emporia tied the game 14-14 before Harman scored a quick seven points. The Purple was not seriously threatened from that point. No Cat found double figures but Harman, Head and Stone paced the scoring efforts with nine points each. John Dean and Barrett added eight points apiece.

Phillips University (Manhattan): K-State had little trouble as they defeated Phillips University (Enid, Oklahoma) 60-44 in the home opener. The Cats started slowly but managed a 26-15 halftime lead. The advantage continued to grow in the second half as K-State pulled away. Ed Head led all scorers as the sophomore from Los Angeles, California, netted 20 points. Barrett (11) and Langton (10) also nailed double digits for the 2-0 Cats.

The undefeated record would be tested as K-State prepared to embark on a 6,000 mile trip that would match them against five of the nation's top teams in just nine days. The Cats would fly to California to play San Francisco and Santa Clara, return by air to Manhattan, and then board a train for games against St. Louis, Indiana and Long Island University (in Madison Square Garden).

San Francisco (San Francisco): Before 3,000 fans in the Cow Palace, the Dons of San Francisco edged K-State, 55-53. It was the second game of a doubleheader as UCLA had earlier defeated St. Mary's, 61-58. K-State controlled the first half and had a comfortable 30-23 lead at the intermission. That margin was quickly erased early in the second half, and the teams battled until one minute to play. Tied at 53-53, San Francisco's Don Lofgren nailed a 20-footer to give the Dons the lead which they never lost. Lofgren led all scorers with 17 points while Harman (15) and Stone (11) led the Cats.

Santa Clara (San Francisco): K-State was unsuccessful in their second effort on the West Coast, this time losing in the final minute to Santa Clara, 59-56. The game was a carbon-copy of the San Francisco contest. The Cats fell behind early (9-1) but rebounded nicely and led 26-23 at the intermission. The teams battled back and forth in the second half until the final climactic moments. With under a minute to go, Harman scored to give K-State a 56-55 lead but the Broncos responded with two late buckets to snare the victory. Harman (14) and Stone (11) led the scoring.

K-State did receive some good news from back in Manhattan. A new "Touchdown" would grace the sidelines soon! Not a football touchdown. No, this "Touchdown" was a living wildcat that was being trained by Mark Field, a student at the Veterinary School. The new wildcat had been captured in Colorado five years earlier and had recently found a home with the fire department in Hutchinson. Evidently the wildcat had a rather healthy appetite and satisfying that appetite was becoming a bit too expensive for the firemen. Enter Alpha Phi Omega. The K-State chapter purchased the cat for $50 and began preparing him for his new home. This cat was very comfortable around people, yet was hardly tame. Upon competition of extensive preseason training, the new mascot would soon be unveiled!

St. Louis (St. Louis): After a quick trip back to Manhattan, K-State boarded the train and lost to St. Louis University, 51-45. The Billikens, the 1948 National Invitational Tournament Champions, trailed 29-26 at halftime but took the lead early in the second half. The two teams then battled back-and-forth until St. Louis secured the lead for good with just three minutes remaining. Head (13) and Dean (11) paced the Kansas State attack.

Indiana (Bloomington): The Cats suffered their fourth straight loss as Indiana pounded the Purple, 56-36. The Hoosiers avenged a loss that they suffered to K-State in the 1947-48 campaign. The Cats stayed close in the first half but were no match as IU overpowered the visitors to gain their fifth straight win. Shooting woes killed K-State: the visitors managed just 10 of 71 (14.1%) from the field. Harman led the efforts with nine points. Indiana was paced in scoring by Lou

Watson and Bill Garrett, who had 14 and 13 points respectively. Garrett was more than a scoring leader. He also was the first black athlete to play basketball for the Hoosiers.

Long Island (New York City): The road trip ended as K-State lost its fifth straight, this time to Long Island, 63-60. It appeared the Cats would win this game. They held a narrow 30-28 lead at the half but stretched the margin to 50-39 with 10 minutes remaining. The Blackbirds then changed some strategy. Unable to handle K-State's quickness with a man-to-man defense, Long Island switched to a zone. It was now the Cats' turn to struggle. K-State was unable to get inside shots and began to gamble with longer chances, chances that missed. The Blackbirds raced on a 12-0 run and pulled away for the win. Head paced K-State in scoring, netting 15 points. Long Island was led by dazzling Sherman White, who netted 16 points. He would have more big games against the Cats in upcoming years.

The winless road trip was not completely a bust. The Wildcats, with sophomores and juniors doing most of the playing, were painfully learning how to close out a game. It was time to return to Manhattan and apply those lessons.

Iowa State Teachers College (Manhattan): After five straight losses, K-State gained their third win of the season, defeating Iowa State Teachers College (Cedar Falls), 54-47. It was a much tougher game than was anticipated. The Cats raced to a 5-0 lead but the visitors tied the game at 10-10. Kansas State finally took control and had a comfortable 30-24 lead at the half. The lead didn't last long. The guests from Iowa pulled ahead 35-34 and the teams traded baskets until the game was tied, 40-40. Ernie Barrett and Henry Specht provided badly needed points and sparked a 10-4 run which helped the Cats edge away to the victory. K-State shot 32.8% (22 of 67) from the field. Stone (14) and Barrett (11) led the scoring but the play of Specht was crucial. The Piqua, Kansas, native added eight points, most in the critical second half.

Kansas State now set their sights on Kansas City and the third annual Big Seven Holiday Tournament. In addition to the conference teams, Harvard joined the tourney as an invited guest. As defending champion, K-State did not travel to Kansas City at full strength. Rick Harman, who suffered a leg injury during the Indiana game, was hobbled. Harman re-injured the leg in the Long Island contest and did not play against Iowa Teachers College. It was very doubtful Gardner would let the Hoisington junior see any action until he was completely ready.

Nebraska (Kansas City): K-State opened the holiday bash in style, defeating Nebraska, 48-34. The Cornhuskers, one of the league's best offenses in 1948, had major problems against the Cats. K-State opened a 29-15 lead at the half and was not challenged as John Dean (14) led the Purple in scoring. Iowa State, KU and Oklahoma also claimed first-round wins.

Kansas (Kansas City): Kansas overpowered the Cats, 60-46, to move into the finals of the holiday tourney. The Jayhawks jumped to a 5-0 lead and were never threatened. Jerry Waugh paced KU with 18 points while Barrett led the Cats with 10. K-State was also getting some fine play from Eureka native Ward Clark, who scored seven and six points in the two tournament games.

Iowa State (Kansas City): Kansas State finished a disappointing fourth in the holiday tourney, losing to Iowa State 56-52. The Wildcats had the early advantage but the Cyclones tied the game late in the first half and settled for a 26-26 tie at halftime. The Cats surged ahead early in the second half before Bob Petersen, the Cyclones' speedy guard, took over. Petersen, who scored 19 points, was all over the court, controlling the pace of the game with his superb ball-handling skills. He also stole numerous Cat passes and set-up many baskets as well. Head led the Cats with 14 points while Ward Clark continued stellar play, adding 10. Oklahoma nipped KU to claim the tournament title.

Rockhurst (Manhattan): Kansas State closed out the non-conference portion of the season, defeating Rockhurst 50-38. Neither team could find their shooting touch in the first half, as the Cats clung to a paltry 19-13 lead at the intermission. During the closing minutes of the game the Wildcats finally pulled away for the victory. Head (15), Dean (11) and Lloyd Krone (10) led the scoring.

As the Big Seven Conference season approached, K-State was clearly struggling without Harman. The Wildcat junior continued to suffer bad luck at every turn. Harman had not played in the holiday tourney because of an injury to a leg muscle. As game time approached for Rockhurst, he was finally pronounced fit, only to severely sprain his ankle in warmups! Gardner announced that Harman would be sidelined several more weeks.

Missouri (Columbia): K-State opened conference play, losing to Missouri, 49-42. The Tigers were in control in the first half, leading 24-20 at the break. They widened the margin in the second half before the Cats rallied, tying the game at 42-42 with five minutes to play. Missouri, led by Pleasant Smith (who had battled influenza just days prior to the game), responded and scored the final seven points to get the win. Dean and Head led the Cats with nine points each.

As K-State prepared for their conference home opener against Colorado, more news was being made off the court than on. The Cats had no fewer than five players suffering from various injuries. On a positive note, the living wildcat had passed all of his tests and would become the new mascot of Kansas State. Thurlo McCrady, the Director of Athletics, planned to present the 29-pound Wildcat to the fans during the Colorado game. Following in the tradition of Touchdown I, II and III, this cat would be named Touchdown IV.

The Buffaloes boasted two Kansans on their starting five. Bob Rolander (McPherson) and Carr Besemann (Newton) were outstanding juniors for CU. The two, along with Rick Harman, had been high school stars in Kansas in 1946. Rolander and McPherson lost to Besemann and Newton in the Class AA state finals while Harman led Hoisington to the Class A state title. Harman (knock on wood) would be ready for the Buffs. In his career, he had yet to lose to Colorado.

Colorado (Manhattan): Kansas State gained its first conference victory with a narrow 48-43 triumph over Colorado. The Buffs led throughout the first half and entered the locker room up 23-19. In the second half, they widened the margin to as much as nine points before the Purple finally made a move. Head and Krone fueled the comeback, and with less than five minutes to play, forced a 37-37 tie. Colorado enjoyed their last lead (38-37) before Stone and Harman netted points to give K-State a lead they would not relinquish. Head (15) and Krone (13) paced the Cat scoring attack while Harman, back for the first time since late December, netted five points. Rolander paced Colorado with 10 tallies while Besemann was held scoreless.

Iowa State (Manhattan): The Cats won their second conference battle, this time defeating Iowa State, 49-43. After a sluggish start by both teams, Iowa State dominated the first half, forging a 27-21 halftime advantage. K-State responded at the start of the second half and went on a 6-0 run, tying the game at 27-27. From that point, the Cats dominated. K-State held the Cyclones without a field goal for the next nine minutes and opened a commanding 45-33 lead. Fouls became a major concern for the Purple, however, and the Cyclones roared back, cutting the lead to just 45-42. K-State found their form in the end, led by Harman. The junior star from Hoisington scored 13 points, 10 in the final half. His two late buckets secured the victory. Harman was the only Cat in double figures. For the game, Kansas State shot 29.3% from the field (17 of 58).

Oklahoma (Norman): K-State snapped an Oklahoma seven-game winning streak, defeating the Sooners 47-45. The Cats led for much of the game, although OU had one lead, 35-30, at the midpoint of the second half. Once again, Rick Harman was key to the victory. Harman netted 16 points, including key buckets as K-State broke away from a 43-42 deficit to take the lead. OU was hampered by the absence of center Marcus Freiberger, who was unable to play due to the death of his mother. Freiberger, 6'11" tall, was the tallest player in OU history! Despite Freiberger's size, the Sooners' Paul Courty (an all-conference forward in 1948) was still the driving force behind Oklahoma. In the game, Courty nailed 13 points for the Sooners while teammate Wayne Glasgow added a team-high 15 tallies. Harman was the only Wildcat in double figures.

Colorado (Boulder): K-State suffered its second conference loss as Colorado upset the Cats, 48-41. The Buffs raced to a 9-1 lead and were not seriously challenged in the game. K-State was greatly hampered by travel problems. The train, scheduled to transport the team, was delayed many hours and the team did not depart Manhattan until 4:00 a.m. the day of the game. The Cats arrived in Boulder just before the tip off and looked haggard from the opening minutes. K-State mounted several challenges to Colorado, but never drew closer than seven points in the second half. Lloyd Krone led the Purple in scoring, managing 11 points. Wayne Tucker paced the Buffaloes with 16 points while Bob Rolander added 12.

Nebraska (Lincoln): The Cats' road woes continued as they were destroyed by Nebraska, 70-48. It was a close game for a half, as K-State trailed 25-22 at the intermission. As the second half began the Cornhuskers exploded on a 17-7 run and quickly ended any drama. Jack Stone led the Cats in scoring, netting 12 points. With the loss, K-State's conference mark fell to 3-3.

As the Cats returned to Manhattan, big news was awaiting them. Clarence Brannum, Phog Allen's favorite Wildcat, was back for the newly beginning second semester! The former Winfield star had left Manhattan in June due to financial reasons and had been playing AAU basketball for the Peoria, Illinois, Diesel Caterpillar company team. Back on campus, Brannum announced that he intended to finish school whether he could play basketball or not. As it turned out, he had a chance to again play for the Cats. Professor H.H. Haymaker (K-State's Faculty Representative) researched the conference rules and found that Brannum would meet the eligibility requirements, provided he could pass a three-hour final examination. Haymaker informed the press that Brannum had not taken the test prior to his withdrawal from school in June, but was carrying a "B" average prior to leaving. The press was tingling with excitement and raced to get comments from Phog Allen. The KU coach uncharacteristically remained mum! Brannum did take the test and passed, restoring his eligibility. The Cats did lose Ward Clark, however, the dependable 6'5" junior from Eureka. Grade issues would sideline him the rest of the season.

Missouri (Manhattan): Missouri defeated K-State, 40-34, in a tight game in Manhattan. Brannum joined the squad (he scored three points) but his appearance could not counter a fired-up Tiger team. Prior to the game, MU Coach Sparky Stalcup announced that two key Missouri players (Dan Pippin and George Lafferty) would be held out of the game because of an eligibility issue due to their grades. Technically, since the school registrar had yet to officially inform the MU coach to the contrary, the two players would have been eligible for the K-State game. Stalcup decided to err on the side of caution and withheld the players. Pippin was a huge loss. The Tiger forward had been an all-conference selection in both 1947 and 48, and was currently the top scorer in the Big Seven (scoring nearly 12 points/game). The absence of the players (and the appearance of the "suddenly eligible" Brannum) served to motivate MU and they dominated the game. The Cats managed just 15 first-half points and trailed by nine (24-15) at the intermission. The Tigers, despite one serious Cat rally, maintained that lead throughout the final half. Ernie Barrett paced the scoring for K-State, netting eight points.

Wildcats and Jayhawks scrap for a rebound in their meeting in KU's "Tiny" Hoch Auditorium. 'Cats won 53-48. — Courtesy of Kansas State University Archives

K-State now prepared for one of the sternest tests yet: KU in Lawrence! Both teams were having difficult Big Seven seasons. K-State had a record of 3-4 while KU stood at 2-3. Coaches Allen and Gardner both sensed that a win might quickly turn things around as the conference season reached the stretch run. With that in mind, lineup changes seemed in order. KU decided to insert Sonny Enns, a hard-driving guard from Newton. Enns had recently played well, scoring 22 points in the last three KU games. Coach Gardner, in turn, named Clarence Brannum as a starter. The bruising center from Winfield had helped the Cats win two games from the Hawks in 1948.

Kansas (Lawrence): In the 114th meeting between the two schools, K-State defeated KU, 53-48, before 4,000 fans at Hoch Auditorium. The Cats took a brief early lead before the Jayhawks fought back. Midway through the first period, KU led by eight, 16-8. The Wildcats managed to rally and entered the locker room down 26-23 at the halftime break. The second half was a different story. K-State became the aggressor (led by Harman) and pulled ahead with 15 minutes to play. The Cats never lost their grip, despite KU's use of a pressing defense. Harman led the Purple in scoring with 13 points (10 in the second half) while Krone added 12 (eight in the second half). Claude Houchin paced the Hawks, netting 14 points. Clarence Brannum gave Coach Allen few headaches. The big center scored just three points and fouled out with 16 minutes remaining in the game. Despite the win, KU still held a commanding 77-37 record against Kansas State.

Oklahoma (Manhattan): K-State defeated Oklahoma for the second time in the season, edging the Sooners 51-45. It was just Oklahoma's second conference loss, both to the Cats.

Kansas State never trailed in the game and held the Sooners without a field goal for a 13-minute stretch of the first half. The Purple settled for a 24-18 lead at the intermission and withstood two OU second half rallies to gain the win. The contest was extremely rough with a total of 56 fouls whistled (29 against OU). Clarence Brannum led the Cats in scoring with 12 points and, coupled with Jack Stone, held 6'11" Marcus Frieberger, Oklahoma's huge center, scoreless.

Kansas (Manhattan): In a sterling performance, K-State destroyed KU, 63-36, before a capacity crowd that included numerous state legislators. The Cats jumped to a 18-7 early lead and the Hawks never mounted any response the entire game. Harman (20) and Brannum (11) netted double figures as K-State improved its conference record to 6-4. Gene Petersen paced the Hawks with 11 points. With the loss, KU saw its record dip to 3-6 and fell into sixth place in the conference. The Cat's 27-point margin of victory over KU was the second largest in school history. On February 2, 1917, K-State had plastered KU by 29 points (38-9) to establish the record. The students certainly did their part. As the game was quickly settled, the chant "We want a field house" echoed across Nichols. Attending legislators, led by Democrat Elmo Mahoney of Dorrance (brother of current K-State player, Ken), had an answering chant: "You'll get a field house!" It was not just political speak: they delivered!

Just one day later, the Kansas Senate passed a $725,000 appropriations bill. The money was the last hurdle necessary for the building of a new field house. A beaming Jack Gardner was in attendance as the lawmakers concluded their vote. In 1945, the Legislature had appropriated $750,000 as an initial stimulus to build the badly needed structure. In 1947, an additional $300,000 was added to the project. Since that time, construction bids showed that $1,050,000 would still be far from adequate. Thus, an additional $725,000 was earmarked for the construction.

KU would not be left out of the picture. On the same day, several KU basketball players asked for permission for the 1949-50 home games to be moved from Hoch Auditorium to Robinson Gymnasium. The players, in their petition to Chancellor Deane W. Malott, partly blamed the auditorium for their poor performances. They noted that the floor at Hoch Auditorium was built on a concrete base, which increased foot injuries. The petition had one small problem: Hoch seated 4,000 fans while Robinson seated just 2,500. Logistically, the plan would not fly, but that was not the intent. The publicity was designed to increase sentiment for a new KU field house, one bigger and better than the Cats' new palace. If K-State had one, KU would not be left out. With time, the Hawks would also christen a brand-new structure.

Nebraska (Manhattan): On March 1, Kansas State pulled an upset, pounding conference leader Nebraska, 53-28. The Cats never trailed in the contest as Rick Harman nailed 19 points. The Cornhuskers managed only seven field goals for the entire game. The victory threw the Big Seven race into a quandary. With a 7-4 record, the Wildcats were still in the hunt for a share of the conference title, provided they could defeat Iowa State and a series of losses befell both Nebraska and Oklahoma. The Cats' late-season push was drawing some national attention as well. K-State received an invitation to play in a four-team tournament to be held in Cincinnati. The Cats were flattered, but rejected the offer. The Big Seven had long frowned on teams playing in post-season tournaments. Only the conference champion was afforded that honor. Coach Gardner did not ask for an exemption. The conference policy would stand.

Clancy prepares to lower the boom. Clarence Brannum (19) and Barrett (9) work together on maneuver which husked Huskers.
— Courtesy of Kansas State University Archives

Iowa State (Ames): The Cats closed out the season with a 54-39 victory over Iowa State. K-State led 22-17 at the half and pulled away to conclude the season with a 13-11 record (8-4 in the conference). Harman paced the scoring efforts with 15 points. The Cats still held out hope for a share of the conference title, but that honor went to Nebraska and Oklahoma, who tied for the top spot (both with 9-3 records). Nebraska advanced to the national tournament but lost to Oklahoma A&M in the first round. The Aggies from Stillwater would eventually lose the national championship game to Kentucky. With the end of the season, Rick Harman and Lloyd Krone both received all-conference nominations (Harman first team, Krone second team) by the United Press. They both received identical awards from the Associated Press as well. In addition, Clarence Brannum, Ed Head, John Dean and Jack Stone were Honorable Mention selections by the Associated Press.

The season was capped by a spadeful of dirt. On March 19, construction officially began on the new field house. Governor Frank Carlson and more than 4,000 people attended the event. K-State students from various campus organizations outlined the plot of the new structure while a helicopter was scheduled to take photographs of the festivities. High winds grounded the copter but it hardly mattered. The 14-year crusade had finally come to an end! The dream of Mike Ahearn would become a reality with profound effects on Kansas State Basketball for years to come. Tentative plans called for the structure to be completed by December 1950. Bennett Construction Company of Topeka would serve as the contractor for the project.

Team Statistics (Newspaper box scores):

K-State:	1203 points	50.1/game
Opponents:	1146 points	47.8/game

Individual Scoring Leaders (Newspaper box scores):

Rick Harman (Hoisington, Ks.)	188 points	11.1/game
Ed Head (Los Angeles, Cal.)	174 points	7.3/game
Jack Stone (Los Angeles, Cal.)	171 points	7.1/game
Ernie Barrett (Wellington, Ks.)	136 points	5.7/game
Lloyd Krone (Chanute, Ks.)	127 points	5.8/game
John Dean (Harveyville, Ks.)	130 points	5.4/game
Allan Langton (Eureka, Ks)	86 points	3.7/game
Ward Clark (Eureka, Ks.)	57 points	5.2/game
Clarence Brannum (Winfield, Ks.)	38 points	6.3/game
Henry Specht (Piqua, Ks.)	22 points	1.7/game
William Dresser (Oroville, Cal.)	20 points	1.8/game
Glenn Channel (Kansas City, Ks.)	17 points	2.1/game
Ken Mahoney (Dorrance, Ks.)	9 points	1.3/game
Others	28 points	

NCAA CHAMPION: Kentucky (32-2)
RUNNER-UP: Oklahoma State
THIRD PLACE: Illinois
FOURTH PLACE: Oregon State

1950

All is Forgiven in Love & Basketball

Record: 17-7
Conference Record: 8-4 (tie 1ˢᵗ)
Final National Ranking: 14ᵗʰ (AP)
Team Captains: Lloyd Krone & Allan Langton

The varsity squad which produced for Jack was - Back Row: Coach Jack Gardner, Ernie Barrett, Jack Stone, Lew Hitch, Clarence Brannum, Rick Harman, Assistant Coach Tex Winter. Middle Row: John Gibson, Perk Reitemeier, Harold Hauck, Raymond Vawter, Lloyd Krone, Ed Head. Front Row: Snowy Simpson, student manager, Jim Iverson, Dick Peck, Allan Langton, Don Upson. — Courtesy of Kansas State University Archives

As the 1950 season approached, the popular notion among sportswriters was that the Big Seven was Kansas State's to win. With returning veterans Rick Harman, Clarence Brannum, Lloyd Krone, Jack Stone, Ed Head and Ernie Barrett, the Cats were loaded with talented players who could deliver a title. Gardner downplayed the talk, noting that K-State lacked height at the center position. As one surveyed the conference, Gardner's assessment had considerable merit. Oklahoma returned 6'11" Marcus Freiberger, Missouri had 6'9" Don Stroot, Nebraska built its offense around 6'9" Milton Whitehead and Colorado revolved around 6'10" Rod Bell. There also was a certain 6'8-1/2" sophomore from Terre Haute, Indiana, named Clyde Lovellette who now wore a varsity jersey at KU. His height would become a major issue, both on and off the court! These players dwarfed the Cats' 6'5" Clarence Brannum. The Wildcats did have junior Lew Hitch, a 6'8" transfer from Culver-Stockton. Hitch was the tallest Wildcat but did not have the experience that Brannum possessed. Gardner also expected contributions from reserves Dick Peck, John Gibson, Jim Iverson and Allan Langton. Overall, the team lacked size but did have speed and quickness. With 11 games to be played in December alone, the Wildcats would have to gel quite quickly.

Rockhurst (Manhattan): K-State opened the season with an easy drubbing of Rockhurst, 83-34. The point total was a record for the Cats, surpassing the 76 points scored against Kansas Wesleyan on March 3, 1911. The Wildcats jumped to a 11-0 lead and cruised as Barrett (15), Harman (14) and Iverson (12) all scored in double figures. All told, 13 Cats found the scoring column.

Emporia State (Emporia): Before a near-record crowd, Kansas State notched its second victory of the season, easing past Emporia State, 59-50. The Cats enjoyed a comfortable lead early in the game but settled for just a 32-30 advantage at the intermission. In the second half, K-State stretched the lead back to 10 points and secured the victory. Brannum and Harman paced the Cats with 14 and 13 points respectively. The crowd of 4,500 was the second-largest to ever witness a game in the Emporia City Auditorium. Only the state finals of the Class AA high school basketball tournament had drawn a larger crowd. K-State had little time to celebrate as they prepared for a four-game road trip that would take them to Wisconsin, New York and West Virginia.

Wisconsin (Madison): Wisconsin held off an early second-half K-State rally and defeated the Wildcats, 56-48. The Cats trailed 26-22 at the half but quickly recovered in the second stanza and held their last lead, 33-32. Enter Wisconsin center Don "Radar" Rehfeldt. The Badger big man, who led all scorers with 21 points, netted hook shot after hook shot as Wisconsin opened a 50-41 lead, one they would never relinquish. Harman led the Cats in scoring, netting 11 points.

Long Island University (New York City): Ernie Barrett sparked a late second-half rally as K-State defeated Long Island, 58-51. The game, played in Madison Square Garden, was part of a doubleheader, as later that night City College of New York defeated SMU 67-53. The Cats raced to a 16-6 early lead before the towering Blackbirds, led by 6'9" Herb Schere and 6'7" Sherman White, took over. The two scored 14 points helping Long Island to a 31-25 lead at the half. Still trailing with seven minutes gone in the second half, Barrett took over. The "Wellington Wizard" scored 10 straight points and propelled the Cats to 48-40 lead, one they would not lose. Barrett ended the game with 15 points, while Stone and Krone added 11 points each. Leroy Smith, the Blackbirds guard, led all scorers with 21 points. The win was the first K-State victory ever in Madison Square Garden.

Canisius (Buffalo): Canisius, undefeated in four starts, kept their record perfect as they edged K-State, 54-51. The Griffins trailed 28-23 at the half, but used a quick second half explosion to pull ahead. The Cats managed one last gasp, closing a seven-point deficit to just a point, but Canisius made enough free throws to get the win. Brannum (16) and Barrett (11) led the scoring for K-State.

West Virginia (Morgantown): In an upset, K-State defeated West Virginia 49-44. The game was tied at the half, 23-23, but the Wildcats won the game at the foul line, netting 13 charities to just eight for the Mountaineers. Rick Harman poured in 19 points to lead all scorers while Stone added 10. The loss was just the second home defeat for West Virginia in five years!

As the Cats returned home with a big boost of confidence, they received yet another encouraging word. In a recent edition of a college basketball magazine, Kansas State was tabbed as the 17th best team in the country. That ranking nearly mirrored the Associated Press, which had listed the Cats as the number 20 team in the land. In terms of the Big Seven, only Colorado (number five) and Oklahoma (number 15) was pegged higher than K-State. Coach Gardner was quick to ensure that the publicity didn't go to the Cats' heads, however. He labeled the Eastern trip as mediocre and called the Cats "fat and slow!" It was time to flex some muscle.

Baylor (Manhattan): Eager for some payback, K-State avenged the 1948 Final Four loss and humbled Baylor, 78-30. The game was total domination by the Cats from start to finish. K-State held Baylor scoreless from the field for the entire first half and led 30-9 at the intermission. In the second half, when the score

Ernie Barrett is shown hitting a lay-in against Baylor. — Courtesy of Kansas State University Archives

grew to 60-21, the bench took over as the Purple improved its record to 5-2. Four Cats found double figures: Brannum (17), Krone (12), Iverson (11) and Harman (10). For the game, K-State allowed just nine field goals.

The Cats quickly turned their attention to Washington State, who would be entering Nichols Gymnasium in just a few short days. The Cougars held a 5-1 record and were a sophomore-laden squad, led by 6'7" Gene Conley. Conley was rated as the Pacific Coast Conference's "Clyde Lovellette," a big-man who could dominate. Washington State also practiced "two-platoon" basketball, sending in players five at a time. The combination of height, strength and depth made the Cougars a favorite for not only their conference title, but for national honors as well.

Washington State (Manhattan): Showing little regard for the Cougars, Kansas State pounded Washington State 63-39. The Cougars enjoyed one lead, 7-5, before the Cats zoomed to victory. Harman (12) and Brannum (11) led the scoring. Defensively, K-State held Washington State to just 12 field goals. Conley, the huge Cougar center, managed 16 points.

With an impressive record of 6-2, it was time to prepare for the Big Seven Holiday Tournament in Kansas City. Conference teams had fared quite well in non-conference play up to this point. The Big Seven carried a record of 34-14 into the tournament with Colorado a perfect 7-0 against opponents. Michigan was invited to complete the eight-team field and it was generally felt that any of the eight teams could quite easily leave Kansas City with a first-place trophy. The most talked about player entering the tournament was KU's Clyde Lovellette. The Terre Haute, Indiana, "terror," was one of Phog Allen's most celebrated recruits and he had not disappointed, averaging 19.7 points/game. Lovellette, officially listed as 6'8-1/2" tall, was a major obstacle in all phases of the game. His next opponent wasn't just anybody, however: it was Kansas State.

Kansas (Kansas City): Before a capacity crowd, Kansas State rallied in the second half and defeated Kansas, 58-48. The game was THE ticket in KC on the night of December 27! A sellout crowd of 9,500 crammed into Municipal Auditorium, with another 2,000 turned away at the doors. They witnessed a game of two halves. KU dominated the first stanza as Clyde Lovellette scored 10 of the Hawks' first 18 points for a quick 18-9 bulge. Lovellette was too much for Clarence Brannum, as the big Cat center was quickly saddled with three fouls. K-State finally rallied late in the first stanza as Lew Hitch, Brannum's replacement, greatly improved the Cats' chances. At halftime, the Wildcats trailed by just six, 29-23.

The second half belonged to K-State. Brannum, upset and perhaps embarrassed by the big KU center, returned with a vengeance, scoring seven points in quick succession. When the Winfield senior picked up his fourth foul, Hitch returned and continued the pressure. As the Cats began to inch away, KU grew cold, going scoreless from the field for nearly 12 minutes. It was enough for a Purple victory. Brannum and Barrett paced the Cats with 12 points each, while Harman added 10. Lovellette led all scorers with 20. The story of the game, however, was K-State's Lew Hitch. The tall and lean junior from Griggsville, Illinois, scored a career-high nine points and, teaming with Jack Stone, frustrated Lovellette at every turn in the second half. It was the first encounter for Lovellette against K-State. He would more than have his share of moments against the Cats. Oklahoma, Missouri and Colorado also posted first-round wins.

Oklahoma (Kansas City): The Cats were frigid from the opening tap and it cost them dearly as Oklahoma defeated K-State 55-50 in a second-round match. The Sooners trailed early in the game but became inspired by the play of Wayne Glasgow. The OU forward found the groove and the Sooners turned a 14-10 deficit into a 32-23 lead at the half. During the stretch, K-State went nearly seven minutes without a field goal. The second half was much the same as the Cats managed to mount just one serious rally. Glasgow ended the game with 25 points while Barrett led the Cats, netting 16. It would be an unlikely final: Oklahoma and Missouri, a combination few had seriously expected.

Colorado (Kansas City): The Cats powered to a third-place finish, defeating Colorado 59-46. K-State grabbed an early lead and was not seriously challenged in the first half, settling for a 32-24 halftime bulge. In the second half, the Cats hit the Buffaloes with a 10-1 run and settled the matter quite quickly. Brannum had a huge game, scoring 16 points and passing up numerous other chances in order to find his open teammates. Harman chipped in 13. Missouri surprised Oklahoma, 44-42, to claim their first holiday tourney title. KU struggled and finished sixth.

Utah State (Manhattan): Kansas State closed out the non-conference schedule with a 70-45 thrashing of Utah State. The game was tied twice (3-3, 5-5) before the Wildcat power took over. K-State clicked in all phases, including shooting, canning 28 of 81 field goal tries (34.6 %). Barrett led the way, netting 16 points while Harman added 11. Bert Cook led the Aggies with 14 points. He would improve on those numbers in an important K-State game in December, 1950!

As K-State prepared for the conference opener against Nebraska (in Manhattan), the Cornhuskers threw the Cats a curve. Nebraska petitioned the conference to postpone the game. The Big Red complained that the Wildcats had yet to install glass backboards, which had been mandated by the conference office. For its part, Kansas State had ordered the backboards, but were sent the wrong model and had to return them. As a solution, Gardner proposed switching the home games. Instead of postponing the game, Kansas State would simply travel to Lincoln and the Cornhuskers could return to Manhattan at a later date. Nebraska refused. Gardner tried more diplomacy: play the game at a neutral site. Nebraska again would not budge and the conference agreed. The game, originally scheduled for January 7, would instead be played on March 11.

K-Staters smelled a rat! Newspapers across the Sunflower State speculated that Nebraska simply wanted more time before they had to face K-State. If that was the case, the Cornhuskers found the loophole to give them that time. Kansas State now faced a 10-day vacation from basketball. In addition to the unwanted downtime, the Cats received another jolt. Entering the NU game, the AP Basketball rankings had K-State at number 20. Now, with time on their hands, the Cats fell out of the Top 20 rankings completely.

The controversies didn't end for Kansas State. Nebraska's next opponent was a home game against KU. Gardner, in a media interview, was asked how the Cats would deal with being the clear favorite to win the conference title. The Wildcat coach didn't take the bait, and pointed out that all the schools of the Big Seven had the necessary ingredients to win the title. He particularly noted that KU was (in Gardner's opinion) the league's "sleeping giant," and went on to comment that if "Clyde Lovellette was not 7'1" tall, my eyes were getting quite poor at judging height!"

As KU arrived in Lincoln to play Nebraska, a news conference was arranged and Harry Good, the Cornhuskers' coach (with Phog Allen closely watching), officially measured Lovellette. The sophomore star was 6'8-1/2" tall! Allen used the opportunity and uncorked on Gardner. "This boy wonder coaching marvel from Manhattan has developed an uncanny ability of taking old-fashioned and ineligible players and miraculously turns them into amateur college grinds," asserted the KU coach. Phog was just warming up. Most of K-State's squad, according to Allen, consisted of transfers from other schools or athletic organizations. He particularly noted that K-State junior Lew Hitch, a 6'8" transfer from Culver-Stockton College, was just a bit shorter than Lovellette. According to Allen, Hitch was the key backup to "Grandpa Brannum!" "If the K-State coach's vision is as faulty as he confesses," concluded Allen, "it is no wonder that his other special senses plague him continuously. He sees things in the dark and has been suffering from an abnormal case of growing pains these past several years."

The Cats had yet to play a conference game and were already embroiled in what seemed like a full-court assault! A little detective work by K-State found that one newspaper may have slightly "twisted" a Gardner quote from another interview, turning it into something much more derisive of KU and Allen. Gardner at first claimed he had been misquoted but that did little to smooth the waves. No matter how the story was reported, Gardner publicly apologized. The verbal spat, according to the K-State coach, was bad for the conference and his comments were not intended in any way of demeaning KU, Coach Allen or Lovellette. For K-State, it was high time to get out of the newspapers and just play basketball.

Oklahoma (Norman): Kansas State finally began conference play, edging Oklahoma 43-42 in overtime. The Cats trailed at halftime, 19-15, but rallied in the second half and claimed their first lead, 36-35, with two minutes remaining. The Sooners regained the lead, 37-36, before Rick Harman netted a 20-footer to give the Cats the advantage with just 30 seconds left to play. Oklahoma got the last shot and the Sooners' Wayne Speegle knotted the game 38-38 with a last-second free throw. In overtime, OU grabbed a quick three-point advantage before Krone and Harman put the Cats in front to stay. A last-second Sooner attempt rolled off the rim as K-State snapped a seven-game home court winning streak for Oklahoma. Harman led the Cats in scoring, netting 13 points. Wayne Glasgow, who torched the Cats in Kansas City, led OU with just nine tallies.

Iowa State (Manhattan): Setting a new Big Seven scoring record, Kansas State thrashed Iowa State 99-57. The game was all K-State, with the Cats roaring to a 45-26 lead at the intermission. The Cyclones never recovered. Harman (16), Head (11), Krone (11) and Hitch (11) all found double figures. The 99 points scored were the most ever in a conference game, surpassing the 81 points posted by Oklahoma (against Nebraska) in 1948. The game was the 72nd between the two schools with K-State holding a 39-33 edge in the series.

K-State now prepared for a two-game road trip against Colorado and Nebraska. Gardner was not about to have history repeat itself. In 1949, the Cats were delayed in their travels to Boulder, arriving just in time for the game. They proceeded to lose 48-41 to the Buffs. Their efforts two days later in Nebraska brought similar results. Those two losses, for all practical purposes, cost the Cats the 1949 conference title. Gardner took no chances this time: K-State left for Boulder a day earlier.

Colorado (Boulder): K-State showed no effects of their travels west as they whipped Colorado, 75-45. The Cats left the gate quickly and opened a 16-9 lead before the starters began to feel the thin air. Gardner went to his bench and sent in five substitutes (Allen Langton, Ed Head, Lew Hitch, Don Upson and Jim Iverson). Those five powered the Purple to a halftime lead of 40-19. The second half was much the same as the Cats improved their record to 12-3 (3-0 in the conference). Barrett paced the scoring efforts, netting 15 points. Colorado fans were quite certain the game was the worst beating the Buffaloes had suffered in five seasons.

Nebraska (Lincoln): Before nearly 10,000 fans, K-State did not fare quite as well on the second leg of the road trip, losing to Nebraska 65-63 in overtime. The Cats entered the game as the 12th ranked squad in the land (Associated Press). The contest was very tight with the largest lead for either team being a three-point bulge by the Cornhuskers at halftime. In the second half, the two teams traded leads on nearly every possession. Finally with seconds remaining, Rick Harman nailed a free throw to force a 57-57 tie and overtime.

The Purple seemed in control during the extra frame, and led 63-61 with just 30 seconds remaining. A Nebraska bucket knotted the score and K-State played for the game winner. The Wildcat shot missed and the Cornhuskers quickly grabbed the rebound and flung the ball to half-court. The entire arena watched as NU's Bob Gates nailed a 40-foot bomb as the buzzer sounded! Four Cats scored in double figures: Brannum led the way with 14 points, followed by 12 for Stone, 11 for Head and 10 for Harman. The loss produced a three-way tie atop the Big Seven with KU, NU and K-State all posting a 3-1 record.

Oklahoma (Manhattan): In the 67th meeting between the two schools, K-State smashed Oklahoma 91-68. The Cats played poorly for most of the first half, and at one time trailed by 10 points. They finally found their form, paced by Head and Harman, and turned the deficit into a four-point lead (36-32) at halftime. The second half was all Kansas State. They built on the four-point lead as they held the Sooners scoreless for more than six minutes. The Wildcats had outstanding scoring balance as Harman (21), Barrett (19) and Brannum (15) all found double digits. Wayne Glasgow paced the Sooners with 22 tallies. With the win, Kansas State climbed to number10 in the national rankings. Undefeated Holy Cross was still number one while Bradley held down the second spot.

Missouri (Columbia): K-State could not break the "Columbia jinx" and lost to Missouri, 59-43. It was the Cats' 13th straight defeat in Columbia (the last win being a 46-42 victory on February 8, 1937). Despite the Wildcats' high national ranking, Missouri handled K-State with surprising ease. The Purple did lead 21-19 at the half but that lead quickly evaporated as the Tigers clamped down with a stellar defensive effort. How stellar? K-State entered the game averaging 74.2 points/game. They got nowhere near that total as Brannum was the leading scorer with just nine points. The Tigers Don Stroot led all scorers with 17.

K-State had little time to wallow in their defeat as their next game was on Valentine's Night against Kansas. Although KU held a commanding edge in the series, the Cats had won seven of the last eight. KU was paced by Clyde Lovellette, who was leading the conference in scoring, averaging 24.6 points/game. Rick Harman was the only Cat in the top 10 in conference scoring (13 points/game) but K-State clearly had a more balanced attack. The timing of the game was just too rich to ignore. Newspaper columnists wondered what kind of valentine Phog Allen would be sending Clarence Brannum, Lew Hitch and Coach Gardner!

Kansas (Manhattan): In a very rugged game, K-State reclaimed a share of the Big Seven lead by defeating KU, 55-50. K-State trailed for much of the first half before claiming a 29-25 halftime lead. The teams traded baskets early in the second stanza before the Cats broke free with 13 minutes remaining and held on for the victory. Lovellette nailed 20 points to lead KU while Claude Houchin added 10. For K-State, Harman netted 13 points while Stone and Krone each added 11. Brannum added nine points and played well against Lovellette. K-State improved their conference record to 5-2 and with three of the last five conference games in Manhattan, the Cats were the clear favorite to grab the title.

Iowa State (Ames): Kansas State kept driving for the conference title with an impressive 80-56 victory over Iowa State. The Cyclones enjoyed just one lead (9-8) as the Cats pulled away to lead 43-29 at the half. Iowa State never threatened as Barrett (13), Stone (13) and Harman (11) led the efforts. Dudley Ruisch poured in 19 points for the Cyclones, tying the Iowa State single-game scoring mark for a guard.

Ernie Barrett battles for the ball with two Colorado players and Lew Hitch starts in to help him.
— Courtesy of Kansas State University Archives

Colorado (Manhattan): Kansas State whipped Colorado, 74-49, to move closer to the conference crown. The Buffaloes were never in the game and K-State took control after just a few minutes of play. Clarence Brannum led the way with 15 points, while Harman and Stone added 11 and 10 points respectively. With the win, K-State ran its conference record to 7-2, still trailing Nebraska, which sported an 8-2 record. KU, the "sleeping giant," was in third place with a record of 6-3. Everything would be settled in just a few short days, or so people thought!

Missouri (Manhattan): The Cats were dealt a staggering blow as Missouri upset them, 58-55. The Tigers entered the game in last place, but shot like champions, netting 47.8 % of their field goals (21 of 46). K-State managed just 26.1% (18 of 69) from the floor.

The Cats jumped to an 8-1 lead and seemed headed for victory when the Tigers began to assert themselves, particularly in rebounding. With numerous close chances, MU tied the Purple and then pulled ahead, 36-33, at the half. During the second frame, Missouri held the Cats at bay, even after K-State twice had whittled the lead to just a point. The Tigers were paced by Don Stroot. The big center not only led all scorers with 19 points, but held Clarence Brannum to no field goals and just four free throws. Krone (15) and Harman (12) paced the Wildcats.

K-State had now put itself in a tough spot. With a record of 7-3, the Cats were tied with KU and both schools trailed Nebraska, which held an 8-3 conference mark. Next up was KU, the NEW KU! The Jayhawks had ridden all season on the back of big Clyde Lovellette and the Terre Haute sophomore had delivered. Increasingly, opponents swarmed around the big man and took their chances that the Hawks had little else in scoring. Coach Allen finally found that scoring balance as Bill Lienhard, Bob Kenny, Harold England, Jerry Waugh, Bill Hougland, Dean Wells and Claude Houchin were beginning to find their scoring touch.

The rivalry could not be played without off-the-court shenanigans. Both campuses bore numerous "painting projects" but this game took on new significance when KU students successfully kidnaped "Touchdown IV," the K-State mascot, from the Sunset Zoo in Manhattan! A day after the caper, an anonymous KU student gave details to the *Lawrence Daily Journal World*. "A group of us (around 35 students) from KU struck the unguarded wildcat den at the zoo," said the student. "We broke the lock and coaxed the cat into a cage, which we loaded into a car and returned to Lawrence. The cat was rather agitated until we fed it some hamburger and water. It seems to like Lawrence just fine!" The next night "Touchdown IV" was paraded before the KU pep rally, drawing huge cheers before the students who had gathered. Phog Allen himself paid tribute to the daring deed. Noting that in recent days the Oklahoma City Zoo had lost a prized leopard, Allen applauded the students who returned with the K-State mascot. "Oklahoma City officials missed their cue and should have called on these 35 KU boys for help in capturing the escaped leopard," said Allen to the delight of the gathered crowd. The two school student councils were not that enthusiastic about the events, however. They had just recently negotiated a "peace pact" to prevent such an occurrence but clearly the kidnappers had missed the signing ceremony!

Kansas (Lawrence): The Jayhawks dealt Kansas State another near-fatal blow as they defeated the Cats, 79-68. KU hustled quickly to a 22-7 lead before Ed Head led a rally, cutting the halftime deficit to just 36-28. The first-half was the Clyde Lovellette Show as the Jayhawk star had 17 points at the intermission. He finished the game with 32, but the Hawks (those New Hawks) had balance as Claude Houchin nailed 19 and Bill Hougland added 15. Head saved the Cats from utter annihilation. He scored a career-high 24 points while Barrett added 11.

The game was decided at the foul line. K-State was whistled for 32 fouls and KU capitalized, converting 29 of 37 attempts. KU committed 21 fouls which the Cats converted into 16 points. This game was also one for the record books. The 79 points were the most a KU team had ever scored in conference play. The combined 147 points were the most ever scored by the two rivals in a single game. Perhaps even harder to swallow was the fact that the KU point total was the most points any Jack Gardner team had ever surrendered. "Touchdown IV" was returned to Manhattan the day after the game. The mascot, with belly full of food, survived the trip to Lawrence much better than the other Wildcats!

With the loss, K-State had no hope for an outright title but still could claim a tie (with Nebraska and KU) if K-State could defeat Nebraska in Manhattan and the Hawks stumbled in Norman. This was the Nebraska game that had been rescheduled because of backboard problems. The incident had clearly burned at K-State, particularly when the Cats had made several good-faith offers to alleviate the problem. It also was the final home game for seniors Rick Harman, Clarence Brannum, Lloyd Krone and Allan Langton. With a new field house being built just blocks away, a certain gymnasium named Nichols was also making a final curtain call. All of these factors would be part of this final game.

Nebraska (Manhattan): Kansas State edged Nebraska, 63-60, to grab a piece of the Big Seven basketball title. The win, coupled with Oklahoma's overtime victory over Kansas, left K-State, Nebraska and KU tied with identical 8-4 records and the first three-way tie in the conference since the 1940 season. Early signs seemed to indicate that the Cats would not be in that mix. Nebraska opened the game quickly and had an 8-1 lead, holding K-State without a field goal for the first five minutes of the game. The Cats finally got untracked, and hit the Cornhuskers with a 14-2 surge which helped propel them to a 27-25 lead at the half. The second half was close until Ernie Barrett accounted for five successive points to break a 45-45 tie. The Purple never trailed again. Barrett led the scoring with 18 points while Head and Iverson also hit double digits with 12 and 10 points respectively.

The date of this game (March 11, 1950) also had another bit of significance: It was the final varsity game played in Nichols Gymnasium. The gymnasium, named after Ernest Nichols, Kansas State president from 1899-1909, was completed in June of 1910. Over the years the Cats posted a 228-136 record in the gym, a winning percentage of .626.

With the Cat victory (and KU loss), the fireworks began. In a surprising move, the Fifth District of the NCAA selected KU as its representative in the upcoming playoff game against Bradley. The committee, composed of Bruce Drake, basketball coach at Oklahoma, Artie Eilers, Commissioner of the Missouri Valley Conference and C.E. McBride, sports editor of the *Kansas City Star*, reasoned unanimously that of the three teams, the Jayhawks were playing the best basketball at the end of the season and were most qualified to represent the conference. Eilers and Drake had met in Norman immediately following the KU game and then called McBride with their decision. McBride concurred and KU was designated to represent the conference.

Gardner was furious with the decision, labeling it "the greatest injustice ever done to a bunch of fine athletes." He filed an appeal with the committee and began to make his case. First, K-State had the best overall record (the Cats were 17-7, Nebraska 16-7 and KU 14-10). Second, K-State had split its two games with Nebraska while winning two of three from the Hawks. Third, K-State had already defeated both Baylor (the Southwest Conference representative in the District Five Playoffs), and Washington State, the playoff finalist for the Pacific Coast Conference. Fourth, the conference was ignoring precedent. In past instances, the offense-defense ratio (points scored against points allowed) had been used to settle ties. During the season, K-State scored 1,535 points and gave up 1,240. The point differential (295 points) strongly favored the Cats. Fifth, K-State had a higher national ranking than either KU or NU. Finally, Gardner appealed for his seniors, whom he felt were being accorded a "great injustice." The committee heard the appeal but it was really just a formality. Gardner knew he had little chance for a reversal and he was correct. KU was going and the issue was closed. Nebraska, for its part, had remained rather quiet during the ruckus. When pressed for a comment, Cornhusker Coach Harry Good felt Nebraska (the defending Big Seven Champion) was the logical pick to settle the tie. "We were co-champions in 1949 and this season we are on top again," said the NU boss. "Our team is made up of more veterans and I feel we would give a better performance in the playoffs than Kansas." Good, unlike Gardner, did not file an appeal to the decision. Phog Allen accepted the decision, adding "had the invitation been tendered to one of the other teams, KU would have accepted the committee's decision and extended best wishes to that school as they prepared for Bradley."

K-State fans were not so quick to let the issue drop. A group of students drove to Kansas City and marched straight to the desk of *Kansas City Star* sports editor C.E. McBride. The group, carrying signs and becoming rather animated, protested the decision to award KU the playoff game. Newspapers around the conference were outraged at the display and publicly criticized both Coach Gardner and Kansas State President Milton Eisenhower for fanning the students' sentiment.

Gardner said no more. He was being courted by both Northwestern and Michigan State for coaching positions and paid a visit to the East Lansing campus personally. He would stay in Manhattan. The K-State student body returned to their normal, daily routines, but not without one last gesture of sportsmanship. On the day of the KU-Bradley playoff game, the K-State student council sent a telegram to KU: "To Dr. Allen and the KU team: We extend our sincere wishes for a victory over Bradley. All is forgiven in love and basketball. Play the ball you are capable of, and congratulations to the NCAA champions to be." The telegram was signed by Rick Harman, representing the student council. Newspapers around the conference were not impressed. Most felt that K-State should have immediately sent such a letter once the selection of KU was official. Gardner and Eisenhower endured a second round of criticism for the conclusion of the season. The Jayhawks played well but narrowly lost to Bradley, which ended up as the national runner-up to City College of New York. For the New York school, it was the "grand slam" of basketball. Just weeks earlier, they also defeated Bradley for the National Invitational Tournament title. CCNY became the first and only school to win both titles in the same year!

Harman, Brannum, Krone and Langton ended their varsity careers as one of the finest graduating classes Kansas State had ever produced. As a class, they helped win 66 games while losing 34. While they attended K-State, the Cats won or shared two conference titles. They also helped lead the school to its first Final Four appearance. Clarence Brannum was named a First-Team All Big Seven Selection in 1950, while Krone, Barrett and Harman were second team choices. Ed Head and Jack Stone were honorable mention selections as well.

Several other accolades fell to Harman. The Wildcat senior earned All-American honors from a number of publications including being chosen by *The Sporting News* as a member of their 1950 "First Five All-Star Team." Harman was just Kansas State's fourth All-American, joining F.I. Reynolds (1917), Frank Groves (1937) and former teammate Howie Shannon (1948). The *Topeka Daily Capital* also reported that the Hoisington senior left Kansas State as the school's all-time leading scorer. Harman ended his career with 820 points, surpassing Frank Groves, who finished his career with 631 points in three seasons of varsity play. Harman also was credited with another school record. The Wildcat star snared 18 rebounds against Oklahoma in the 1949 season, the most by any Wildcat in a single game.

It was a disappointing and controversial ending to the season, but bigger things were just days ahead. A palatial field house was nearing completion and very talented players were returning, anxious to play in the new building. Great things were expected of the 1951 season and great things were exactly what Kansas State fans would get!

Team Statistics (Newspaper box scores):

K-State:	1535 points	64.0/game
Opponents:	1240 points	51.7/game

Individual Scoring Leaders (Newspaper box scores):

Rick Harman (Hoisington, Ks.)	271 points	11.2/game
Ernie Barrett (Wellington, Ks.)	241 points	10.0/game
Clarence Brannum (Winfield, Ks.)	231 points	9.6/game
Jack Stone (Los Angeles, Cal.)	148 points	6.2/game
Lloyd Krone (Chanute, Ks.)	148 points	6.2/game
Ed Head (Los Angeles, Cal.)	109 points	6.8/game
Lew Hitch (Griggsville, Ill.)	99 points	4.1/game
Jim Iverson (Mitchell, S.D.)	65 points	2.9/game
Allan Langton (Eureka, Ks.)	64 points	2.7/game
John Gibson (Pittsburg, Ks.)	53 points	2.2/game
Dick Peck (Anderson, Ind.)	47 points	2.1/game
Don Upson (Arkansas City, Ks.)	45 points	2.0/game
Others	14 points	

NCAA CHAMPION: City College of New York (24-5)
RUNNER-UP: Bradley
THIRD PLACE: North Carolina State
FOURTH: Baylor

1951
10-Star Attack

Record: 25-4
Conference Record: 11-1 (1st)
Final National Ranking: 3rd (UPI) & 4th (AP)
Team Captain: Ernie Barrett

Back Row (left to right): Head coach Jack Gardner, Ernie Barrett, Arnold Droge, Lew Hitch, Dick Knostman, assistant coach Tex Winter. Middle Row (left to right): Joe Condit, John Gibson, Perk Reitemeier, Dick Peck, Dan Schuyler, Ed Head, Jack Stone. Front Row (left to right): Snowy Simpson, Don Upson, Bob Garcia, Bob Rousey, Kay Coonrod, Jim Iverson.
— Courtesy of Kansas State University Archives

As the summer of 1950 unfolded, excitement about Kansas State basketball was reaching new heights for more than one reason. Fans were naturally "pumped" for the upcoming season, given the returning talent of Ernie Barrett, Jack Stone, Ed Head, Lew Hitch and Jim Iverson. There also was soon to be the debut of a certain sophomore from Wamego named Dick Knostman who had Cat fans counting the days until the season began.

There was yet another reason for Kansas State to anticipate the basketball campaign. For more than a year, residents of Manhattan had watched the campus landscape. Slowly but steadily, stone by stone, the long-awaited field house was rising from the area just north of the football stadium. The magnitude of the edifice was incredible. The field house was the fifth-largest such building in the United States and easily the largest state-owned building in Kansas. The floor area was larger than a football field with the peak of the roof 84 feet above the playing floor. The fans were paramount in the planning: 5,400 fans could be seated in the balcony alone, and when the portable bleachers were moved in, the seating expanded to 13,400. Next to the field house would be a separate gymnasium housing three basketball floors, locker rooms, wrestling and boxing rooms, a training room, coaching offices and classrooms. The gym would be completely finished in March 1951. As for the field house -- well, it had a date with destiny: December 9, 1950. That was the day Utah State would invade Manhattan to play the Cats in the first game ever in the new building. Although not every seat would be installed, and some paint would be applied later, the fans hardly cared. The 1951 season was going to start in grand fashion.

KU was not to be left out of the media attention. The Lawrence campus announced plans for a $1.5 million field house and was quick to mention that their structure would be big enough to contain the entire Kansas State field house! The Hawks expected their project to be completed in two years.

Kansas State was not without some turmoil, however. At the close of the 1950 football season, Coach Ralph Graham resigned. It was not a great surprise, but five days later there was one. Athletic Director Thurlo E. McCrady announced his decision to step down as well. McCrady had replaced Mike Ahearn. The resignation caught everyone off guard. Kansas State made it clear that they hoped to hire two separate people for the two jobs. There would be no double duty for the football (or basketball coach). With the round ball season set to commence, there was more than a field house under construction in Manhattan in November 1950.

Despite all of the off-court news, basketball was still to be played. The United Press issued its first college basketball poll, with City College of New York as the top team in the land. Bradley, Kentucky, North Carolina State and KU rounded-out the top five. The Cats entered the season ranked number 12. K-State would quickly be tested as they embarked on a three-game Eastern road trip, with stops in New York, Ohio and Indiana. With the return of Barrett, Head and Stone, the Cats had three experienced regulars from the 1950 team, co-champions of the Big Seven. John Gibson, Dick Peck, Lew Hitch, Don Upson, and Jim Iverson also were returning lettermen. The big "if" for Kansas State was the center position. Clarence Brannum had graduated and although the 6'8" Hitch had ably backed-up Brannum, he was being pushed by Dick Knostman, a sophomore from Wamego. In the freshman-varsity game, Knostman led the varsity with 17 points. To be successful, K-State needed points and rebounds from the center position. It was hoped that Knostman, Hitch or both would step forward and provide them.

Long Island University (New York City): Before 14,500 fans at Madison Square Garden, Kansas State lost to Long Island University, 60-59. The Blackbirds, a preseason number seven choice of the United Press, held a four-point lead (29-25) before the Cats opened strongly in the final period. With the game tied at 36-36, it appeared the visitors were ready to take control but Long Island went on a 11-0 run, putting the Cats in a huge hole. Kansas State rallied, led by Jim Iverson, and cut the lead to just one, 60-59, with 15 seconds remaining, but the Blackbirds managed to hold the ball until the final gun to gain the win. Iverson led the Cats in scoring with 19 points while Sherman White, an All-American player in 1950, led Long Island with 15 points. In just two months the teams would meet again and White would easily top that point total!

Ohio State (Columbus): Kansas State evened its record at 1-1 with an impressive 68-51 pounding of Ohio State. The game was extremely tight in the first half with the Cats nursing a 35-32 lead at the intermission. K-State had a decided height advantage, however, and that proved to be the difference in the second half as the Purple cruised to the win. Kansas State so dominated the inside game that of their 27 field goals made, 19 were scored inside the lane. Head and Knostman led the Cats in scoring with 16 and 10 points respectively.

Purdue (Lafayette): The Cats gave a second command performance as they defeated Purdue, 60-44. The Boilermakers were a young team and on several occasions had five sophomores on the floor at once. Despite their youth, they stayed with the Wildcats for the first ten minutes of play before K-State gradually began to inch away. Up 27-20 at the half, the Purple took control immediately in the second stanza and coasted to the win. Barrett paced the Cats with 12 points.

K-State now returned to Manhattan and a date with the new field house and Utah State. Let the festivities begin! Coach Gardner had two Kansas State teams whose members he especially wanted in attendance for the game: the 1906 and 1940 teams. Basketball had its first beginnings at K-State in the 1902-03 school year. That team, which compiled a record of 0-5, had no coach. J.W. Fields, Arba Ferris, W.A. Boys, Frank Bates, Earl Evans, A.B. Gahan and Frank Campbell comprised the squad. Fields and Ferris, both now living in McPherson, provided information to Gardner about their "humble" beginnings. Practices were held outdoors and only in the coldest of days did the team practice in the Armory. That building had a 10-foot high ceiling with two-foot beams supporting the roof. Baskets were nailed to these beams, making the goals eight-feet high! The "Aggies" (as K-State was called) played two home games. One (against Haskell) was played in the on-campus hay barn, while the other game was played in the livestock sales pavilion. The team was winless but according to Fields made money for K-State. At the conclusion of the season, Fields turned over the surplus money to Professor J.O. Hamilton, faculty advisor, who commented "This is the first athletic team at Kansas State to ever make money!" No games were scheduled from 1903 to 1905.

The 1905-06 season was Kansas State's first official team. That squad, coached by C.W. Melick, posted a 6-9 record. The '06 team lost games to Campbell, Glasco Athletics, Glasco High School, Washburn (twice), Emporia State, Nebraska, Fort Riley and Ottawa. Wins included games against Minneapolis High School, Fort Riley, St. John's Military, Clay Center High School, Emporia State and the Kansas State faculty. Members of the '05 team in attendance at the Utah State game were Charles Gaine, Burlingame; George A. Dean, Manhattan; Clifford Carr, Kansas City, Mo.; Arba Ferris, Conway; Lawrence Haynes, Wamego; and Charles Topping, Buffalo, New York.

The other honored squad was Gardner's first, the 1940 team. Those in attendance were Ted Garrett, Shawnee; Norris Holstrom, Lombard, Illinois; Jack Horacek, Tulsa; Chris Langvardt, Dodge City; Ernie Miller, Parsons; Ervin Reid, Independence; Joe Robertson, Brownstone, Indiana, and Frank Woolf, Wichita. Both teams were honored with a noon luncheon, the pregame meal of tea and toast with the '51 team, and introductions during the halftime ceremonies.

Two points coming up as Ed Head sends one bucket-bound at the opening game in the new Fieldhouse against Utah State. — Courtesy of Kansas State University Archives

Utah State (Manhattan): Not to be forgotten, there was a game to be played, and the Cats delivered, defeating Utah State, 66-56. Wildcat fans had plenty of anxious moments. K-State started the game ice cold from the field and had to withstand the amazing shooting skills of the Aggies marksman, Bert Cook. In the first half, the Wildcat shooting was in the freezer. With Cook burning the nets, the Cats clung to a 30-26 lead at the intermission. The second half was equally close, with K-State never able to separate itself from the Aggies until the final four minutes of play. Cook personally kept Utah State close, as he nailed buckets from all corners. Despite being only 6'2" tall, the Utah State star dominated the boards as well. Dick Knostman proved to be the key for the Cats, scoring 11 second-half points to finally help secure the victory. Knostman led the Purple with 17 points while Cook nailed 26 to lead Utah State. The field house construction was not quite complete. Several sections of bleachers had yet to be installed. Additional seating would be added in the coming week, just prior to the showdown with the undefeated Indiana Hoosiers. Despite the limited seating, a record crowd of 10,500 jammed the new field house to attend the contest. This was the largest crowd ever to witness a basketball game in the state of Kansas.

Wichita (Manhattan): The Cats had little trouble with Wichita, defeating the Shockers 73-42. The game hardly started as a high-scoring affair. After nearly three minutes of play, Wichita had zoomed to a 2-0 lead! Ed Head finally hit two free throws, knotting the game. With the lid off the basket the Cats powered to a 31-18 lead as they went to the locker room. Wichita drew no closer as Knostman (15), Barrett (13), Head (12) and Iverson (11) found double digits. The Shockers were led by Johnny Friedersdorf, who netted 11. He had been averaging 21 points/game. The showdown with Indiana was next. The Hoosiers were ranked number 10 in the most recent United Press poll while K-State held the number nine spot.

Indiana (Manhattan): Before a record crowd of more than 11,000 fans, Indiana defeated Kansas State 58-52. The Cats again started the game frigid from the field, going without a field goal for nearly six minutes of play. That lull was enough as the Hoosiers jumped to a 14-6 bulge and never trailed. K-State was down five (34-29) at the half, but with Indiana star Bill Garrett on the bench in foul trouble, crawled back to within one, 45-44, with seven minutes to go. Back came Garrett and the senior star delivered down the stretch. He led all scorers with 15 points while Knostman (12) and Iverson (10) found double digits for the Cats. K-State had little time to lick its wounds. Big 10 power Wisconsin was roaring into Manhattan.

Wisconsin (Manhattan): In perhaps their best game of the young season, K-State smashed Wisconsin, 77-58. The Wildcats wasted little time and quickly jumped to a 7-0 lead. That margin ballooned to 40-21 at the intermission as the Cats nailed 17 of 35 field goals (48.6%) in the first half. The Badgers were never able to recover. Stone (14), Iverson (13) and Bob Rousey (11) paced the scoring efforts for the Purple.

In attendance for the game was a very interested guest, KU Coach Phog Allen. A story was reported that at halftime, a student-aged fan approached the Jayhawk and asked for his autograph. Allen graciously obliged and then watched as the fan took a match to paper and burned the autograph on the spot!

Springfield College (Manhattan): Kansas State routed Springfield College (Massachusetts), 82-59. Once again, the Wildcats had a bumpy beginning, going nearly six minutes without a field goal. At the intermission, the Purple held a slim 28-23 lead. The second half was all Wildcats as John "Hoot" Gibson took charge. The Pittsburg, Kansas, guard led a quick-strike attack, and before seven minutes had elapsed, the Cats had opened the lead to 16 (45-29). The Maroons had no answers as K-State hit the Christmas break with a record of 6-2. Gibson led all scorers with 16 points while Rousey, Stone and Knostman each netted 10 points.

As Christmas carols filled the air, the new field house was like the gift that kept on giving. After only five home dates, 44,500 fans had already attended. By contrast, in 1950 the total attendance at Nichols Gymnasium for the entire season (10 home games) was 30,000 fans. With more seats yet to be installed, attendance numbers would only grow.

After a few short days of holiday festivities, the Cats were back in practice, preparing for the 5th annual Holiday Tournament in Kansas City. In addition to the conference family, the Minnesota Gophers joined the tourney as the invited guest. Kansas, the highest ranked team in the conference (number four nationally), was the early favorite to claim the title.

Oklahoma (Kansas City): In a nail-biting game, the Cats defeated Oklahoma, 55-53, to win their first-round game at the holiday tourney. K-State reversed the course of previous games and started quickly. Several times in the first half they led by 12-points and seemed destined to run the Sooners out of the gym. Oklahoma hung on, however, and pulled to within eight points (28-20) at the half. The second half was completely different as OU, led by future KU Coach Ted Owens, crawled back into the contest. After forcing a tie at 47-47, the two teams battled back-and-forth until Charlie Pugsley split the Cats defense for a lay-up, forcing the last tie at 53-53. With a little more than one minute to play, Kansas State delayed for a final shot and Jim Iverson, the Cat junior who also pitched for the baseball team, tossed a perfect strike with just one second remaining and netted the winning bucket. Owens paced the Sooners with 12 points while Hitch and Barrett led the Cats with 14 points each. Iverson and Rousey each added 10 tallies as the Wildcats advanced into the second round.

The other first-round games had their share of excitement too. Clyde Lovellette, the sensational KU junior, poured in a tourney record 30 points as the Hawks pounded Iowa State. He enjoyed the record for all of two hours! Maynard Johnson, Minnesota's fine center, poured in 38 points as the Gophers defeated Colorado. Johnson and Lovellette would battle in second-round action.

Nebraska (Kansas City): Kansas State had little trouble as they pounded Nebraska, 72-53, to gain entrance into the tourney finals. The Cornhuskers had surprised a fine Missouri team in the first round, but this game had little suspense as K-State controlled the contest from the outset. The Cats trailed just once (2-0) and had easily outdistanced Nebraska at the half, leading 36-19. In the second half, the Cornhuskers managed to draw within seven points on several occasions, but got no closer. Lew Hitch netted 14 points but the story of the game was Ernie Barrett. The "Wellington Wizard" poured in 21 points, the most points ever scored in the holiday tourney by a guard. In the other semi-final action, Minnesota collared KU, 62-51. The contest was very physical as Minnesota battered Clyde Lovellette around the floor. The big center still scored 24 points. Maynard Johnson led the Gophers with 23 points. After the game, the rough play brought a swift response from Phog Allen. Asked about the contest, Allen hotly retorted "They murdered Lovellette under the basket." Pressed for more quotes, Allen shut the faucet off and kept any specific officiating comments to himself. KU would grab the third-place trophy the next night. For his part, Lovellette nailed 82 points in the three-game tourney. This total set a new record.

Man of the Hour Coach Jack Gardner rides on the shoulders of his championship Wildcats after the Pre-Season Tournament in Kansas City. Winning this tournament proved to be a good indication of Kansas State's later successes. — Courtesy of Kansas State University Archives

Minnesota (Kansas City): Kansas State became the first team in the conference to win two holiday tourney titles as they defeated Minnesota, 70-62. It was the finest shooting effort of the season as the Cats nailed 27 of 51 field goals (52.9%). The two teams battled on even terms for the first seven minutes of the game. The Gophers, netting a bucket from All-American candidate Whitey Skogg, took their last lead at 14-13 before the Cats powered ahead, led by Stone and Barrett. The two combined for 34 points (Stone 20, Barrett 14) and also did masterful jobs on defense. The Cats forged a 44-37 halftime lead and were never seriously challenged to the end. In addition to Barrett and Stone, Hitch and Iverson each added 11 points in the victory.

Gardner demonstrated some new defensive strategy to deal with the Gophers' dynamic duo, Skogg and Johnson. Each was guarded man-to-man while the other three Wildcats played zone. Skogg still managed 22 points but Johnson, who had scored 61 points in the first two games, was held to just 14 points by the impressive Cat defense. In the end, Gardner was quite pleased with the Wildcat effort. "We knew we had to stop two players," said the Cat boss. "Skogg was terrific but we managed to slow them down and it was just enough."

Kansas State left Kansas City as the ninth-ranked team in the country and riding a serious wave of momentum. The tourney had demonstrated a prevailing trend, not only in the Big

Seven, but also around the country: the zone defense. Increasingly teams were using the defense, packing defensive players inside the free throw line, and daring opponents to beat them from the outside. K-State was one team well suited to handle a zone. Barrett, Iverson, Rousey, Head and Upson could more than "deal" from the perimeter. All the stars and planets seemed in alignment for this K-State team to do something very special.

Missouri (Columbia): Kansas State opened the regular portion of the Big Seven season with a 60-43 victory over Missouri. It was a monumental win. It was the first time a Wildcat team had defeated the Tigers in Columbia since 1937! The game was tied 29-29 at the intermission before the Cats opened the second half on a 7-0 run. It was a prelude to disaster for the Tigers, who shot a paltry 8.33% (three of 36) from the field in the second stanza. Stone (20), Iverson (13) and Barrett (12) paced the Cats in scoring. Off the court, the Wildcats had more good news. Ed Head, injured in the opening game of the holiday tourney, was fit to return to the lineup. Despite the winning performances, his presence had been missed.

Iowa State (Manhattan): The Cats continued to cruise, pounding Iowa State 98-58. The game was as easy as the score might indicate. With 16 minutes remaining in the first half, K-State held a narrow 10-7 lead. In the next four minutes, that lead had grown to 26-9 and the rout was on. At halftime, the margin had swollen to 53-27 and even set a record. The 53 points were the most ever scored in the first half by a Big Seven team. Bob Rousey nailed 13 points to lead the scoring, while Hitch and Barrett added 12 points each. Stone (11), Upson (11) and Iverson (10) also hit double digits as 12 Cat players found the scoring column. Up next, a trip to Lawrence.

Kansas (Lawrence): The Wildcats used all of their nine lives and nipped the Jayhawks, 47-43. The game matched the Cats' balanced attack against the immovable force, big Clyde Lovellette. The KU center scored 17 points in the first half as Kansas State clung to a 24-19 lead. In the second half, KU found some balance of their own and with seven minutes remaining, led 42-36. Back came the Purple with both Barrett and Hitch providing the points. With just 45 seconds remaining (and the game tied at 43-43), Barrett nailed the decisive bucket (a 30-footer) to give the Cats the lead. KU came back down the court and missed a chance for the tie, and in the fight for the rebound, Jack Stone, Clyde Lovellette, Jerry Waugh and Sonny Enns became entangled. The pile up resulted in several punches being thrown, the benches emptying and fans spilling onto the court. Order was restored and no players were ejected. Hitch and Gibson led the Cats in scoring with 10 points each while Lovellette tossed in 27. No other Jayhawk was in double figures.

Before the game, the Purple had some extra incentive. Coach Gardner informed the players that Assistant Coach Tex Winter had recruited an additional player who might see action if necessary. Winter than produced a miniature Kansas State jersey tailored to exactly fit Tex's new son Russell, born just one week earlier! After the game, Gardner publicly stated that he hoped KU would be able to build its new field house. The K-State coach felt the melee at the end of the game would not have happened in a bigger arena, one where the fans could not be seated so closely to the floor.

Nationally, one story began to take center stage: the Korean War. During World War II, many service men suspected that some top collegiate and professional athletes were granted deferments when they were more than able to serve their country. Korea was another war and Defense Secretary George C. Marshall made it clear that if an athlete was fit to "suit up," the army would provide that suit! All the coaches of the Big Seven quickly concurred with the Secretary. Gardner, in an interview, summarized their feelings when he stated "No coach should put personal ambitions to build a strong team before the country's needs in time of national emergency. Wars are not won by deferments!"

Colorado (Manhattan): The Cats suffered a letdown from the KU game but still hammered Colorado, 63-42. Although it was not a polished affair, the Wildcats led all the way and were not seriously threatened. K-State jumped to a 11-4 early lead and Colorado never drew closer. The game was marred by one incident, however. Bob Rousey was booted from the game for slugging a Buff player. Eleven Cats scored, led by 15 points from Lew Hitch.

After the game, Coach Gardner acknowledged that Kansas State had asked him to be the new athletic director, provided he gave up coaching. Gardner issued a statement that he appreciated the offer, but would remain as a coach at Kansas State.

Long Island (Manhattan): In a return match-up, the Cats defeated Long Island, 85-65. On a five-game road trip, the Blackbirds' entered the game with a record of 16-2 and had a number four ranking in the country. K-State was number seven in the poll. The Blackbirds were staggering, however. Long Island had lost their two previous games (California and Arizona) and limped into Manhattan. The Cats showed little mercy. The first half was back-and-forth with K-State clinging to a 38-37 halftime edge. The Blackbirds' offense consisted mostly of their star, Sherman White. The All-American had 24 points as the teams hit the locker rooms and at times toyed with his defenders. After a brief flurry by Long Island, the Wildcats finally took over in the second half and raced to the 20-point win. Hitch (20), Barrett (14), Stone (13) and Gibson (12) all found double figures. Hitch also set a new K-State single-game record by grabbing 19 rebounds, one more than Rick Harman had snared against Oklahoma in 1949. The Cats had more success guarding White in the second half. He managed 13 tallies and ended the game with 37 points. After the game, Gardner felt White was one of the finest players the coach had ever seen. It was the swan song for White, however, as in the next few days a major scandal would not only engulf college basketball, but would also draw White into it.

Earlier in the year, KU had traveled to New York City to play St. Johns University at Madison Square Garden. While in the Big Apple, Phog Allen used the opportunity to propose some rule changes to the game. He also expressed a growing concern with gambling on college basketball games. Just prior to the K-State game against Long Island, Allen again blasted Eastern basketball, saying there were "plenty of rotten eggs in the bunch." Long Island Coach, Clair Bee, was not overly impressed with the head Jayhawks' comments. Speaking to the Manhattan Quarterback

Club the day of the K-State game, Bee took some swipes at Allen. He felt Allen was (once again) using the New York press to grab some attention. Bee also was not that concerned about gambling. "It is not the one dollar bet between friends that is bad," said Bee. "When a gambler wants to get a cinch and tries to bribe a player, that is when the thing should be stopped." As it turned out, Allen knew exactly of what he spoke. The problem was much bigger than just small wagers and, in fact, had crossed the most dangerous of lines: point fixing! During the week of January 20, 1951, arrests began to be made. Several members of the 1950 Manhattan (New York) College basketball team were the first to be charged. Those "rotten eggs" that Allen had alluded to were now beginning to make a stink that the entire country would soon smell.

Colorado (Boulder): After the convincing victory over Long Island, Coach Gardner was concerned about the Colorado game in Boulder. He feared a letdown, and his fears were well-founded. The starters struggled, but fortunately the Cats' depth came through and K-State defeated the Buffaloes, 60-45. The Wildcat offense never found a rhythm in the game. Gardner turned to the bench and Ed Head, Bob Rousey and Dick Knostman provided the tonic, helping the Cats to a 29-22 lead at the half. K-State held that lead throughout the second half and posted their 11th straight win. Head ended the game with 14 points while Rousey added 13 tallies. Knostman netted seven points, and combined with his savage work on the boards, helped keep the Purple in front. Colorado's record fell to 4-14 while K-State stood at 15-2.

As K-State traveled to Lincoln for a date with Nebraska, good news came from Manhattan. The school named Larry "Moon" Mullins as its new athletic director. Mullins, the Head Coach at St. Ambrose College in Davenport, Iowa, was a star fullback on Notre Dame's national championship teams of 1929 and 1930. He also had served as head football and basketball coach at St. Benedict's College (now Benedictine College) in Atchison. His 1949 St. Ambrose football team was undefeated and Mullins was named coach of the year for that accomplishment.

Nebraska (Lincoln): Kansas State continued its winning ways, pounding Nebraska 79-50. The Cats, ranked seventh in the country, opened quickly to a 16-4 lead and never were seriously challenged by the Cornhuskers. K-State again featured balanced scoring. Dick Knostman paced the efforts, netting 15 points while Barrett and Gibson added 12 points each. Media around the conference were impressed with the Cats. They possessed many players who could lead the scoring on any given night. One paper dubbed the Wildcats a "10-star attack." Gardner hoped his "10 stars" continued their impressive efforts.

With the win, Kansas State continued to climb in the national rankings. The Wildcats, now listed as the number four team in the land, were riding a 12-game win streak. It was not hard for Cat fans to begin to "think ahead." What they saw in the future was potentially disturbing, particularly to Coach Gardner. The Big Seven Conference, stung by the criticism that Kansas had been awarded the right to play in the national tournament after the three-way tie of 1950, had a new and creative way to resolve any more ties: a coin flip! Gardner was infuriated, calling the method "drastically unfair." The best way to resolve any tie was a playoff, something Gardner had long advocated. "The boys work so hard in an effort to make the national tournament and then their fate is decided by a flip of a coin," protested Gardner. The conference paid little attention to the Wildcat general. For Cat fans everywhere, the surest way to keep the coin in the conference's pocket was for the Cats to just keep winning.

Missouri (Manhattan): Before 12,800 fans, the Cats improved their conference record to 7-0 with a 75-64 victory over Missouri. K-State again demonstrated its depth, utilizing a two-platoon system to overwhelm the Tigers. The first half was tight with the Cats missing numerous scoring chances. Still, they managed a slim 41-34 lead at the intermission. The contest was settled quickly in the second half as K-State hit Missouri with a 25-8 run. Only late scoring by the Tigers kept the final score respectable. Rousey (12), Gibson (12), Stone (11) and Knostman (10) all scored in double figures.

With a 13-game winning streak and a number four national ranking, the Cats were reaping individual honors as well. Ernie Barrett was named to *The Sporting News* "Eight-Man All-Star Team." He joined Clyde Lovellette of KU and Sherman White of Long Island University. White was also named the national player of the year. The award to the Long Island star would become problematic in just a few short days!

Oklahoma (Norman): The Cats' winning streak ground to a halt as Oklahoma upset K-State, 49-46. The Sooners used a full-court press and continually frustrated the offensive rhythm K-State tried to develop. Yet, the first half ended with the Cats leading 27-23. The second half saw quick changes, all by Oklahoma. Marcus Freiberger, the 6'11" center, personally accounted for nine early points as the Cat lead evaporated. Down 41-30, K-State finally countered and drew within two points (48-46) with less than two minutes to play. The Purple had four separate possessions, all to tie the game, but misfired all four times as Oklahoma survived and got the win. Freiberger ended the game with 21 points, while Ted Owens added 11 tallies. Jim Iverson was the only Cat in double figures, netting 11 points.

Nationally, the gambling scandal, first thought to be an isolated incident, was isolated no more. Six players from the national champion City College of New York were charged with being actively involved in both throwing certain games, and accepting bribes to influence the outcome of other games. At San Francisco University, former stars Frank Kuzara and Don Lofgras both admitted that gamblers had tried unsuccessfully to get them to accept bribes and fix games. They refused the offers. Other players and teams were being investigated. It was clear the scandal had grown beyond New York. The United States Senate planned congressional hearings, chaired by Democratic Senator Estes Kefauver of Tennessee.

Three Long Island University players were arrested and charged with "fixing" games, including the K-State game, played in Madison Square Garden on December 2. Although the Blackbirds won 60-59, the bookmakers had set the point spread at eight points. Sherman White, the LIU star who just weeks earlier scored 37 points in Manhattan, also admitted to taking bribes. His name was withdrawn from All-American honors. *The Sporting News*, which just days earlier had named him the player of the year, was stuck. Their issue had already been printed and shipped prior to the new developments. Kansas State President James A. McCain ordered the college athletic council to begin a thorough review of all away games, particularly those in Madison Square Garden, or any other road games not under the complete control of college officials.

Locally, K-State had their usual big game with rival KU upcoming, this time in a sold-out field house. The Oklahoma loss had placed the Cats in a dangerous position. With a conference record of 7-1, they lead KU (6-2) by just one game. A Wildcat loss would knot the two atop the conference standings. Feelings between the two schools were at a fever pitch when Phog Allen tossed out something extra to raise the temperature a few degrees: spying!

Allen made two allegations. First Jack Carby, a former KU basketball player who transferred to K-State, was seen attending several KU games early in the 1951 season. The KU coach found it odd that the young sophomore, who left KU due to academic problems, found attending KU home games so necessary. Second, Allen alleged that at halftime of the January 15 game in Lawrence, one K-Stater (wearing a purple "K" letter sweater) positioned himself outside of an open window in the KU locker room, listening to the KU coaches' every word. As the second half began, the Wildcat "detective" was seen sitting on the Kansas State bench. When Gardner was asked to address the charges, the K-State coach said "I have no idea what he is talking about and I doubt very seriously if he knows himself what he is talking about!"

Kansas (Manhattan): Kansas State steam rolled KU, 65-51, assuring themselves of at least a tie for the Big Seven Title. KU seemed fueled by the spy controversy and raced to an 8-0 lead. The Cats countered and by halftime held a slight 36-33 advantage. In the second half, the Wildcats made their move and stretched the lead to 45-34. They held the margin to the end. Lovellette netted 19 points to lead all scorers while Head, Hitch and Barrett each pitched in 12 points apiece.

A record crowd of more than 13,000 fans attended and those without tickets tried every trick in the book to gain entrance. One brilliant attempt took place before the game. A middle-aged man raced breathlessly up to the ticket booth and announced that he was a game official, had forgotten his pass and was running late. The game would be delayed if he was not admitted! It was a nice try. After the game, the KU bus was delayed for several minutes. Clyde Lovellette was besieged by admiring fans clamoring for an autograph. Despite the loss, the big center graciously obliged and no Lovellette autographs were reportedly burned!

Nebraska (Manhattan): Kansas State won the Big Seven Title and the automatic NCAA bid by defeating Nebraska, 74-48. The Cats, fourth-ranked nationally, had an easy time with the Cornhuskers and won their 19th game in 22 starts. Jack Stone paced the Purple scoring with 17 points, followed by Head (12), Iverson (12) and Barrett (11).

With the automatic NCAA bid secured, the Big Seven Conference Faculty Representatives granted Kansas State the right to play two additional games as preparation for the playoffs. The Cats had unofficially sent feelers to Indiana, Notre Dame and Illinois, anticipating a favorable decision from the conference. Gardner also hoped that KU might be one of the games. The Jayhawks would provide the sternest possible test for the Wildcats, and also would make it possible for fans to see the two teams play again. Dutch Lonborg, Athletic Director at KU, left the decision to Coach Allen and the team. The answer was a emphatic "no." Coach Allen, although wishing to help the Cats, noted that several basketball players would miss valuable time from spring football practice. The KU players voted, and the vote was 17-0 against the game. Allen proposed that in the future, the conference designate two conference teams to play the champion in post-season matches to keep the title-winner sharp for the playoffs. He further proposed that these games be of the "practice variety" and not count in the standings. Gardner was disappointed, but moved on and, after considerable negotiations, Illinois agreed to come to Manhattan to play the Cats.

Iowa State (Ames): Kansas State continued to roll, pounding Iowa State, 81-47, raising their conference record to 10-1 and their overall mark to 20-3. The Cats led throughout and were never challenged as Stone (18), Barrett (14) Hitch (11) and Knostman (11) all netted double figures. Next up for the Wildcats was a rematch with Oklahoma, the only team to beat K-State in conference play.

Oklahoma (Manhattan): Kansas State exacted some sweet revenge, destroying Oklahoma, 87-48. The Sooners were unbelievably cold in the first half, managing just three of 23 field goal attempts (13%) and a paltry 11 points. With a 38-11 bulge, Gardner substituted freely in the second half. Iverson (18), Barrett (13), Knostman (12), Stone (10) and Rousey (10) led the scoring. Marcus Freiberger, the OU center, led all scorers with 22 points.

K-State had received permission to play two games prior to the NCAA playoff but only a battle with Illinois would take place. The Fighting Illini would be a great test. Not considered much of a threat, Illinois surprised everyone and captured the Big Ten Title with a 19-3 overall record.

Illinois (Manhattan): Kansas State tuned up for the playoffs with an impressive 91-72 thrashing of Illinois. The first half was played at a blistering pace with the Cats on top, 51-46, at the intermission. Illinois had considerable travel problems getting to Manhattan and as the second half unfolded, they looked strained from the trip. The Wildcats quickly settled any doubts and continually beat the Illini to every loose ball and rebound. In his last home game at Kansas State, Jack Stone carved his name in the Wildcat record book. Stone netted 29 points, a new single-game school record. His point total surpassed the 28 points scored by both David Weatherby (1946) and Frank Groves (1937). Ernie Barrett also played his last home game, netting 21 points.

The NCAA playoff was next. The Western Regionals (played in Kansas City) featured K-State, Arizona, San Jose State, Brigham Young, Oklahoma A&M, Montana State, Texas A&M and Washington. In the Eastern Regional (played in both Raleigh, North Carolina and New York City) Villanova, North Carolina State, Kentucky, Louisville, Columbia, Illinois, Connecticut and St. John's would battle. K-State and BYU were considered slight favorites in the Western Regional while Kentucky and Illinois garnered the most attention in the Eastern Regional.

As the Western Regional teams gathered in Kansas City, a bit of levity (or embarrassment) took place at a sportsmanship luncheon sponsored by the American Legion. The 1951 sportsmanship recipient was Colorado. Oklahoma, the 1950 award-winner, presented the Buffs with the trophy. In comments during the presentation, Oklahoma Coach Bruce Drake noted that when he informed the OU president about being selected for the '50 award, Drake received "the nicest letter he ever received as a coach, nicer even than the letters he received from Kansas University last year for my work on the NCAA selection committee." Drake, it will be remembered, was a crucial member of the three-man committee which choose KU to represent the conference in the playoffs after KU, K-State and Nebraska had tied for the title. In attendance, Phog Allen was noticeably uncomfortable with the remarks. Gardner retaliated nicely, however, and in his statements noted that it was great to be in Kansas City "on our own merits!"

Arizona (Kansas City): K-State advanced in the playoffs, but just barely, narrowly defeating Arizona, 61-59. The Cats were heavy favorites and for most of the game, looked the part. Kansas State left the gate quickly and by halftime had a comfortable 36-20 lead. The margin grew, and midway through the second half, the Cats led 54-33. Gardner, sensing a chance to rest the starters, inserted the second five and watched as Arizona powered back into the game. With the lead at just 60-49, the starters reemerged, but by now, the desert Wildcats were on a significant roll and continued to nibble at the lead. With great precision, Arizona cut the lead to just one (60-59) but the Purple held on to gain the win. Barrett provided the final point on a free throw as K-State fans breathed a sigh of relief. Head and Hitch were the only two Cats in double figures, netting 13 and 12 points respectively. There was plenty of second guessing of Gardner after the game. Many felt the Cat boss had made a tactical error removing the starters with a 21-point lead. The second team was badly outplayed and suffered greatly when John Gibson hurt his ankle and had to leave the game.

Brigham Young (Kansas City): K-State had some anxious moments, but advanced to the Western Regional Finals with a 64-54 victory over BYU. The game was a repeat of the Arizona contest. K-State jumped to a commanding lead of 39-21 at the intermission. That lead grew to 43-23 early in the second half and the rout seemed certain. For the next eight minutes, however, Brigham Young outscored the Cats 22-6. Now it was a game. The Wildcats found just enough answers down the stretch and claimed the victory as Rousey (13), Head (11), Stone (11) and Barrett (10) paced the scoring efforts.

Oklahoma A&M (Kansas City): Kansas State powered to the national championship game with a commanding 68-44 victory over Oklahoma A&M. The game started like the previous two. The Cats raced to a 37-14 halftime lead, but this time K-State continued the torrid pace in the second half, dominating all phases of the game. Hitch, Knostman and Stone led the efforts with 12, 11 and 10 points respectively.

In the Eastern Regional, Kentucky narrowly defeated Illinois, 76-74, to advance with Kansas State to the national championship game held in Minneapolis, Minnesota. Kentucky was the number one team in the country and K-State was not in the best of shape entering the game. John Gibson had suffered a twisted ankle in the Arizona game and was questionable. Don Upson, the Cat guard, was bothered by a stiff back from the Oklahoma A&M game. Both of these players were key reserves. THE injury, however, involved a starter. Ernie Barrett had hurt his shoulder in the A&M game, and although x-rays were negative, the pain was not. Barrett could barely lift his arm. It was not a good sign as the two Wildcat teams squared off for the national crown.

Kentucky (Minneapolis): Before a crowd of 15,438 fans, Kansas States' hopes for a national title faded in the second half as Kentucky defeated the Cats, 68-58. The first half was a fine effort for the Purple. Lew Hitch and Jack Stone both played exceptionally well, and at the intermission the Cats clung to a 29-27 lead. It all changed in the second half. Kansas State went nearly nine minutes without a field goal and the damage was done. The Wildcats had no answer for 7'0" Bill Spivey, the All-American Kentucky center. The big man netted 22 points and grabbed 21 rebounds. The injury to Barrett, though not an excuse, was clearly a factor. The Wellington senior nailed just two of 12 floor shots and ended the contest with four points. After the game, Barrett could barely remove his warm-up jacket. Stone closed out his career, leading the Wildcats with 12 points. No other Cat scored in double digits.

Post-season honors were many for K-State. Ernie Barrett was named a First Team All-American while Jack Stone was an Honorable Mention selection (United Press). Barrett and Lew Hitch were First Team United Press All-Big Seven selections while Stone was a second team choice. Bob Rousey was the United Press Outstanding Sophomore. The Associated Press chose Barrett, Stone and Hitch as First Team All-Big Seven selections. Earlier in the year, Barrett also had been picked to *The Sporting News* "Eight-Man All-Star Team." One other award graced Barrett. He was chosen to the College All-Star team that would conduct a tour around the country, playing the Harlem Globetrotters.

The 1951 season was a magical time for basketball at Kansas State. If not for one nine-minute drought (and a shoulder injury to Barrett), K-State might have claimed the national championship. Still, a new field house and a terrific "10-star attack" insured that the 1951 team would live forever in Kansas State history. No better team has ever worn the purple!

Team Statistics (Newspaper box scores):

K-State:	1996 points	68.8/game
Opponents:	1546 points	53.3/game

Individual Scoring Leaders (Newspaper box scores):

Ernie Barrett (Wellington, Ks.)	298 points	10.3/game
Jack Stone (Los Angeles, Cal.)	278 points	9.6/game
Jim Iverson (Mitchell, S.D.)	259 points	8.9/game
Lew Hitch (Griggsville, Ill.)	258 points	8.8/game
Dick Knostman (Wamego, Ks.)	217 points	7.5/game
Bob Rousey (Anderson, Ind.)	190 points	6.6/game
Ed Head (Los Angeles, Cal.)	181 points	7.0/game
John Gibson (Pittsburg, Ks.)	158 points	5.4/game
Dick Peck (Anderson, Ind.)	67 points	2.6/game
Don Upson (Arkansas City, Ks.)	46 points	1.7/game
Dan Schuyler (Anderson, Ind.)	21 points	0.9/game
Perk Reitemeier (Lafayette, Ind.)	10 points	0.9/game
Others	13 points	

NCAA CHAMPION: Kentucky 32-2
RUNNER-UP: Kansas State
THIRD PLACE: Illinois
FOURTH PLACE: Oklahoma A&M

1952
Every Man a Wildcat

Record: 19-5
Conference Record: 10-2 (2nd)
Final National Ranking: 6th (UPI) & 3rd (AP)
Team Captain: Jim Iverson

K-State Wildcats were (back row) Snowy Simpson, Gene Stauffer, Jim Smith, Dick Knostman, Jack Carby, Jesse Prisock, John Gibson, Dan Schuyler, Laurence Morgan. (front row) Jack Gardner, Ron Peterson, Gene Wilson, Dick Peck, Bob Rousey, Jim Iverson, Don Upson, and Keith Lambert.
— Courtesy of Kansas State University Archives

Kansas State fans viewed the 1952 basketball season with some trepidation. The 1951 team had just missed out on a national championship and gone from that team were stars Ernie Barrett, Jack Stone, Lew Hitch and Ed Head. The impact of their play and the team's success was noted in one interesting statistic. In 1951, Kansas State led the nation in attendance as 146,000 fans viewed 13 home games. The 1952 team was hardly void of talent, however. Not with Dick Knostman, Jim Iverson, John Gibson and Bob Rousey returning. The four players had seen considerable playing time in 1951 and were strong candidates to start. K-State also returned letter winners Dick Peck, Dan Schuyler and Don Upson. The key for the Cats would be the development of junior Jack Carby and sophomores Gene Wilson, Jesse Prisock and Gene Stauffer. Wilson, a guard from Anderson, Indiana, was one of the quickest players the Cats had ever recruited and was nicknamed "The Jet." Carby was an early positive sign for Gardner. The 6'7" transfer from KU was practicing quite well and if he continued to progress at the center spot, Gardner could move Knostman to the foward position. The first inkling of success came as the varsity clubbed the freshmen, 108-44. Carby, Stauffer, Prisock and Wilson all played well in the easy victory.

As the '52 season approached, the college basketball scandal was still in the news. Newspapers around the country were filled with speculation about the latest rumors involving notable players. In early November, Judge Saul Streit of New York began to try to put some closure to the scandal. The judge, ignoring the pleas of defense attorneys, sentenced five former players to jail for accepting bribes. One of those players was Sherman White, the dazzling star from Long Island University. Streit also gave suspended sentences to another nine players from City College of New York and Long Island University. The "game fixer," Salvatore Sollazzo, was sentenced from eight to 16 years in prison for offering the players bribes. In his sentencing, the judge scolded colleges for "creating a cheap and false collegiate environment to operate basketball as a big business." Some of these players, noted the judge, were unqualified students who had matriculated to the campus through fraud and very probable forgery.

Kentucky, the reigning national champion which defeated K-State in the '51 title game, stood tall in the basketball world, seemingly immune from all of the problems associated with the game. Earlier, legendary Wildcat Coach Adolph Rupp had boldly proclaimed that "gamblers couldn't touch my boys with a ten-foot pole." He could not have been more wrong! In October of 1951, investigators arrested former Kentucky stars Alex Groza, Dale Barnstable and Ralph Beard. All were members of the fabulous 1949 national championship team. The three were charged with accepting $500 bribes to shave points in the NIT Tournament in 1949. Their sentences were later suspended but Judge Streit placed the three on indefinite probation and barred them from sports for three years. The University of Kentucky had taken a first hit. It was just the beginning.

Purdue (Manhattan): Before more than 12,000 fans, Kansas State opened the '52 season by defeating Purdue, 67-51. The Boilermakers stayed close well into the second half before key buckets by Iverson, Knostman and Carby finally secured some breathing space for the Cats. Carby and Iverson paced the scoring efforts with 11 points each. The game was largely a success, although Coach Gardner noted that lineup changes could be expected as the Wildcats prepared for their second Big Ten foe, Ohio State.

Ohio State (Manhattan): K-State blasted a fine Ohio State team, 78-54. The Buckeyes were highly regarded and touted their fine sophomore, Paul Ebert, for early season honors. The young forward did not disappoint, scoring 18 points and snaring 22 rebounds! He was the only Buckeye in double digits, however, as three Cats paced the Purple fortunes. Prisock (12), Knostman (11) and Wilson (10) led the victors with Knostman also grabbing 10 rebounds.

Kansas State now prepared to hit the road with games against Arizona, California and San Francisco on the itinerary. The Cats had played well in both the Purdue and Ohio State games but those contests were in Manhattan. Arizona figured to be another story. The Desert Wildcats carried an amazing 81-game home court winning streak. Arizona no doubt also remembered their 61-59 defeat to K-State in the Western Regionals just nine months earlier.

Arizona (Tucson): Kansas State pulled off a major shocker as they defeated Arizona, 76-57, stopping the Desert Cat home winning streak at 81 games. The streak had begun in 1945. Once again, Kansas State's depth proved to be the deciding factor as four Wildcats notched double figures. Jack Carby, quickly developing as a force at the center position, led the Cats in scoring with 18 points, while Iverson (16), Knostman (11) and Rousey (10) also notched double digits. The victory was by far the most impressive of the young season.

Bob Rousey drives for two! — Courtesy of Kansas State University Archives

As the Purple continued on the Western road trip, big news came from Kansas City. The Big Seven Faculty Representatives, attending their annual meeting, announced some major changes in the conference. The gambling scandal had stunned the entire nation and now it was time for some strong medicine. Effective September 1, 1952, the conference declared that it would ban all post-season competition, including bowl games in football and the NCAA basketball playoffs. Although other conferences followed suit, most of the Big Seven coaches and athletic directors were stunned by the forceful measures. Prior to this, only the Ivy League had banned post-season football play, but that league did allow its basketball teams to participate in the NCAA playoffs. There still was a chance the league could be persuaded to follow another course of action. The coaches and athletic directors hoped that the NCAA, also studying the post-season issues, might recommend a less severe approach.

One other ruling caught the attention of Big Seven basketball coaches. In addition to a post-season ban concerning the NCAA playoffs, the conference ordered that basketball schedules be reduced to a 21-game season, and that practice could not begin any earlier than November 1 (prior to this, practice had begun on October 15). Gardner was not pleased with any of the new rules, particularly the reduced schedule. He noted that the new restrictions would limit teams to just six non-conference games and many of those teams demanded "home and home" contracts. If just three non-conference games could be held at home each year, it hardly would be fair to the fans and would under-utilize the beautiful new field house on the K-State campus.

Initially, Phog Allen was supportive of the new rules. He felt the ban on NCAA playoff games was necessary to curb the money influences that were increasingly permeating the college game. Allen also had little concern about fewer regular season games. The new K-State field house was a huge recruiting advantage for Gardner and with fewer games at K-State, Allen was sure the new rule "would strongly impact my friend up the river in Manhattan!" When informed that practices could not begin before November 1, Phog changed his tune. "Setting practice back to November 1 is asinine—that is a good word, asinine," said the KU skipper. "All other sports are allowed to practice early but basketball practice is reduced. It is just asinine!"

California (Berkeley): Kansas State remained undefeated as they edged California, 64-50. The Bears enjoyed an early lead but the Cats rallied late in the first half to forge a 25-25 tie as the teams went to the locker room. K-State moved ahead in the second half as Bob Rousey nailed nine key points late in the game to preserve that lead and ultimately win the game. Rousey ended the game with 14 points while Knostman added 11 tallies.

San Francisco (San Francisco): K-State suffered its first loss of the season as San Francisco mounted a late rally and nipped the Cats, 55-52. The Wildcats held a slim lead late in the game when Carby fouled out with less than seven minutes to play. His absence provided the Dons with their best opportunity and they capitalized, going on an 8-0 run to gain the lead, 51-45. The Cats rallied and cut the lead to just 53-52, but San Francisco milked the clock and tallied the final two points to get the win. Iverson and Knostman led the Purple in scoring, each netting 11 points.

As K-State returned from the West Coast, more gambling bombshells were expected. Based upon new information, New York officials were visiting the University of Kentucky for a second time. The "ten-foot pole" Adolph Rupp had defiantly proclaimed as the protector of Kentucky basketball was quickly being sawn into much smaller pieces.

Denver (Manhattan): In an error-ridden affair, K-State trimmed Denver, 65-55. The game was by far the poorest Cat effort. Kansas State was out rebounded by the Pioneers but managed to find a way to gain the victory. Jesse Prisock led the Cats with 14 points while Knostman and Wilson each added 12. Denver had played KU a week earlier and was pounded, 84-53. Despite the closeness of the K-State game, Denver Coach Hoyt Brawner felt the Cats were the better, all-around Sunflower State team. He even went so far as to say, "Lovellette did not impress me much!" There was little doubt that his comments would find a prominent place on bulletin boards in Lawrence!

Hamline (Manhattan): Kansas State easily destroyed Hamline, 92-73. The small college from St. Paul, Minnesota, was very highly regarded, having already defeated BYU and Drake earlier in the season. The Pipers had an impressive record of 396-77 in the previous 20 years and had circled the Kansas State game as a real benchmark outing. It turned out to be a benchmark outing for the Cats! By scoring 92 points, the Wildcats set a school record for most points scored against a non-conference foe, topping the 91 tallies posted against Illinois in March, 1951. The game was over quite quickly as the Purple raced to a 27-7 lead and cruised to the win. Prisock (14), Rousey (12), Knostman (11) and Carby (11) all posted double digits in the victory. The Cats' record stood at 6-1 and they now were ranked number five in the Associated Press poll.

Indiana (Bloomington): Kansas State blew an eight-point lead in the closing minutes and lost to Indiana in overtime, 80-75. The Cats, leading 70-62 late in the game, decided to stall the remaining moments of the contest. Bad idea! The Hoosiers, paced by their ball-hawking guards Sam Miranda and Sam Esposito, quickly turned errant Wildcat passes into points and the game ended in regulation as a 70-70 tie. In the overtime, Indiana gained the lead and Miranda and Esposito demonstrated great ball-handling skills as K-State chased them in desperation. The Cats had no answer for Hoosier freshmen, Don Schlundt. The 6'9" center scored 28 points and personally helped to send Carby and Prisock to the bench with foul troubles. Dick Knostman had an outstanding game, netting 26 points to lead the Cats. Iverson (14) and Rousey (10) also found double figures. Iverson was 10-10 from the foul line.

The gambling scandal generated another huge story as Kentucky All-American Bill Spivey, who had scored 22 points against the Cats in the '51 national championship game, was suspended by the Kentucky Athletic Board at Spiveys' request. Spivey was named as one Kentucky Cat who was under investigation by New York officials. The big center denied any wrongdoing and the Kentucky school announced that once the 7'0" star had cleared his name, he would be welcome to return to the Wildcat squad.

Kansas State prepared for the upcoming Big Seven Holiday Tournament in Kansas City. Stanford University joined the conference family in the tourney with KU and K-State the clear headliners. As the Cats prepared to depart for Municipal Auditorium, Coach Gardner announced that four freshmen would be traveling with the varsity. They were 6'11" Jerry Jung of Hutchinson; 6'8" Gary Bergen of Independence, Missouri; 6'4" Nugent Adams of Kansas City, Missouri; and 6'4" Jim Smith of Brainerd, Minnesota. With the Korean War in full swing, freshmen again were granted immediate varsity status. Newspapers across the state had marveled at these freshmen, by far the tallest in K-State history. They had been impressive in their junior varsity outings and Gardner had hoped all season to combine K-State speed with overwhelming size. The four yearlings certainly fit the part.

Nebraska (Kansas City): K-State pounded Nebraska, 87-67, to open the Big Seven Tourney. The Cats got off to a wobbly start but after several anxious minutes, began to click and quickly pulled ahead to stay. The 87 points were a tournament record, surpassing the 85 points scored by the Cornhuskers against Iowa State in 1949. Dick Knostman led the Cats with 17 points while Carby (15), Iverson (11) and Jim Smith (10) also netted double digits. Nebraska was led by their sensational guard Jim Buchanan, who paced all scorers with 25 points. In attendance at the game was Lt. Rick Harman of the United States Air Force. Harman, the former Cat basketball star, was on Christmas leave. Despite the scoring record, the overall K-State effort was hardly impressive as the Wildcats committed many turnovers. They would need to improve all aspects of their game for their second opponent: the undefeated number-four ranked Kansas Jayhawks!

Kansas (Kansas City): In the 121st meeting between these two rivals, KU nipped K-State 90-88 in overtime. Twice in the first half, KU posted a 19-point lead and seemed destined to run the Cats back to the hotel. They settled for a 49-35 halftime lead. K-State clawed back and finally tied the game at the buzzer, 80-80, as John Gibson miraculously tipped in an errant Wildcat shot.

In the extra frame, Clyde Lovellette and Bob Kenney kept the Hawks in front, and when Jack Carby fouled out (and was assessed a technical foul for complaining about the call), KU seemed primed to ease into victory lane. Not so fast. Buckets by Prisock and Knostman knotted the game at 88-88 before KU nailed the final two points to secure the win, the 691st victory for Phog Allen. Kansas had five players in double figures. Lovellette led all scorers with 27 points while Bob Kenney (22), Dean Kelley (14), Bill Lienhard (10) and Bill Hougland (10) found double figures. K-State had six players score in double figures. Prisock and Rousey each netted 15 tallies while Knostman and Carby added 13 points each. Gibson (12) and Iverson (10) rounded out the Cat scoring leaders. Kansas State suffered another shock after the game. Bob Rousey suffered a chest bruise late in the game and as he was departing Municipal Auditorium to return to the hotel, collapsed and was rushed to a Kansas City hospital. It was later determined he suffered a rupture in a lung and would be sidelined for a few days.

Oklahoma (Kansas City): The Wildcats struggled but defeated Oklahoma, 84-69, to capture third place in the tourney. The Sooners stayed close throughout the game. Late in the final half, the Cats clung to a six-point advantage before a 12-0 Wildcat run turned the narrow lead into a much more comfortable margin. Knostman (17), Prisock (14), Iverson (13), Carby (12) and Don Upson (11) all scored in double figures. Kansas won the championship with a 75-65 victory over Missouri. It was their first holiday tourney title.

Arizona (Manhattan): Fresh from the Big Seven Tourney, Kansas State used an early blast to defeat Arizona, 78-52. The Cats raced to an early nine-point lead and were not seriously threatened in gaining the win. Arizona was completing a disastrous five-game road trip, one that saw the Desert Cats lose all five. The Purple's early success came from Jesse Prisock, who opened the game with 10 quick points. He ended the contest with 20 points while Knostman (13), Rousey (13) and Iverson (11) also netted double digits.

The excellent play of Prisock, a native of Emporia, was expected. The 6'5" forward was a highly-recruited talent who had struggled as a freshman in Manhattan. Playing center at Emporia High, Prisock averaged 18.6 points/game as a high school senior. At K-State, he was shifted to a forward position and had some early struggles. With each passing game, however, Prisock was becoming more comfortable at the new spot.

Nebraska (Manhattan): The Cats opened Big Seven play with a 71-36 blasting of Nebraska. The Wildcats jumped to a 5-0 lead and were only threatened once by the Cornhuskers. Leading just 9-8, K-State held the Big Red scoreless from the field for eight minutes and the one-point lead grew to 17 (30-13). The game was over at that point. Jim Iverson paced the scoring with 23 points while Knostman (15) and Gibson (10) also netted double figures. Knostman also set a Kansas State record as he nabbed 21 rebounds, surpassing the 19 grabbed by Lew Hitch in a game against Long Island University (January 31, 1951). For Nebraska, shooting woes continued. In several previous games, the Cornhuskers had found the nets unfriendly, but this game was a new low: Nebraska attempted 95 shots but managed to hit just 15, a meager 15.8%.

Oklahoma (Norman): K-State gave a lethargic effort but escaped Norman with a 65-54 victory over Oklahoma. In the first half, OU hit 50% of their shots, grabbed more rebounds than the Cats, and generally played like they cared! Still, the Cats clung to a 36-30 lead at the intermission. Finally in the second half, Gardner found some hustle as Iverson, Wilson and Gibson helped pull the Purple to victory. Iverson led the Cats in scoring, netting 15 points while Knostman (13) and Wilson (10) followed closely behind. Knostman again had a fine game on the boards, snagging 13 rebounds.

Knostman's play was critical to any Wildcat success. Always an accomplished scorer (he totaled 1,342 career points at Wamego, including a 42-point blast against Council Grove in 1948), Knostman had worked at becoming a better rebounder, and his totals were impressive. The Wamego junior was highly recruited out of high school but there was little doubt that he was a K-Stater from an early age. His father was a center on the 1921 Cat squad while his mother and two sisters also graduated from Kansas State.

Iowa State (Manhattan): Kansas State continued to cruise, defeating Iowa State 76-58. Although it was an easy win, the Cats did have to overcome a nine-minute scoreless drought from the field, one of the longest stretches in recent K-State history. They did manage to hit seven free throws during that period, however, and kept the Cyclones at bay. Two Wildcats did the bulk of the heavy lifting. Knostman led all scorers with 25 points while Iverson added 22.

Next up for K-State was the second-ranked Kansas Jayhawks. What would a KU-K-State game be without some controversy? This time Coach Gardner supplied that very thing! In an interview, Gardner believed it would be hard for the Cats to hold Clyde Lovellette below 25 points, but he hoped to get some help from the officials. Gardner felt Lovellette was getting some preferential treatment from the officials, particularly given his "nudging, bumping and hipping under the basket." As Exhibit A, Gardner noted that in '51 season, the big center averaged four fouls a game, yet fouled out in just 11 of 24 contests. It seemed to continue in 1952. In the recent Big Seven Holiday Tourney contest against KU (won by the Hawks, 90-88 in overtime), Gardner was perturbed that Lovellette had four fouls by halftime, yet played the entire second half and part of the overtime before being whistled for the final offense. "I wish my boys could play as long and get as rough as Lovellette," said the K-State mentor. "How can the radio announcers tell who gets charged with a foul? After Lovellette is assessed with his third foul, every time the whistle blows on the Jayhawks, all the KU players raise their hands like a grade school arithmetic class! It is obvious there is a reluctance to call fouls on Lovellette."

Reached in Lawrence, Phog Allen was hardly amused. "I am not the least surprised," said the KU coach. "I have definite inside information that Coach Gardner has been attempting to improvise a way to influence the officials to get Clyde out of the ball game this week. This is the sinister method he chose."

Phog Allen was not the only person upset with Gardner's comments. Moon Mullins, K-State's Athletic Director, also was angered. "I don't like the comment," said Mullins. "This isn't good for sports or for K-State." Mullins indicated that he planned to discuss the matter with Gardner. Reeves Peters, conference commissioner of officials, also weighed into the fray. He termed the Gardner statements "regrettable" and noted that to the officials, "names of players meant nothing."

All-American Clyde Lovellette of Kansas gets off one of his hook shots over the outstretched hand of K-State's Jack Carby (41). The Wildcats trounced the Jayhawks, Big Seven and NCAA basketball champions, 81 to 64 before a capacity crowd of 13,000 fans.
— Courtesy of Kansas State University Archives

Kansas (Manhattan): In a show of Purple power, K-State pounded the Hawks, 81-64. KU, 14-0 entering the game, stayed close for the first half, trailing only 40-36 at the intermission. The Wildcats' speed, however, took over in the second half and the Cats quickly opened a 17-point spread. KU had little left and fell to defeat. Lovellette played his usual stellar game, netting 31 points and grabbing 16 rebounds. He was nearly matched by Knostman, who scored 27 points a pulled down 16 boards. K-State had a terrific effort from Gene Wilson. The sophomore guard zipped up and down the court, scored 15 points, and played some outstanding defense. Iverson also netted double digits, adding 11 points. It was Gardner's 11th win against the Hawks.

After the game Gardner was ecstatic about the win but downplayed the verbal war waged between himself and Phog Allen. "People have taken this way too seriously," said Gardner. "Phog and I exchange these barbs every year, just like the spy issue last year. The game needed a little build-up. Nobody was hurt by it. I meant nothing malicious. I do, however, stand by what I said but there's no use kicking it around. We got a fair treatment tonight."

The game was a prelude to what most newspapers saw as a real possibility: KU and K-State tied for the conference title. Up to this point, a tie would have likely been decided, not by an actual coin-flip (as was feared) but rather "by lot" (teams drawing straws, choosing numbers or the like). Now the league fathers had second thoughts. Maybe a playoff was the best way to settle a tie. At the upcoming Big Seven Faculty meetings in late February, the idea would again be presented. If a game was needed, it most likely would be played in Kansas City.

Kansas State, with the win over KU, climbed to the number two ranking in the country and was basking in the glow of the rarified air. That was about to change. *The Omaha World-Herald* reported that K-State had violated new recruiting rules involving two Omaha high school players, Stan Schaetzle and David Bell. Specifically, the University of Nebraska filed a formal complaint that K-State had broken two rules. First, the Cornhuskers contended that K-State Assistant Coach Keith Lambert contacted the boys during a "no-contact period." Second, K-State brought Schaetzle, Bell and a third Omaha player (David Pritchard) to Manhattan and held a tryout with the boys, a practice attended by both Lambert and Coach Gardner. Holding a practice (or tryout) was a specific violation of conference rules and after the weekend, both Schaetzle and Bell enrolled at K-State for the upcoming spring semester. Pritchard, so the story went, did not have a good "workout" and was not offered a scholarship.

Athletic Director Moon Mullins tried to put on a good face. In a lengthy statement, the Wildcat boss defended the boys' trip to Manhattan and offered proof (phone conversations and assorted memoranda) that K-State had shown diligence in its contacts with the players. Mullins did admit, however, that K-State could not justify the workout in which the boys participated. The K-State Athletic Council agreed and declared Schaetzle and Bell ineligible until the conference could make a final ruling. K-State President James McCain lauded the council's decision. Despite the media frenzy, McCain felt the council acted immediately (and correctly) in the matter. To McCain, this demonstrated that K-State athletics was under a watchful eye by K-State itself. For now, this issue would rest. In just a few short days however, a new recruiting issue would arise with information from a certain basketball coach in Lawrence.

Colorado (Manhattan): Amidst all of the recruiting controversies, Kansas State had a game to play and the Cats routed Colorado, 92-40. The second-ranked Wildcats had an easy time of it, jumping to a 41-22 lead at the half and then outscoring Colorado 27-8 in the first ten minutes of the final frame to coast to victory. Knostman (19), Prisock (17), Iverson (15) and Carby (11) paced the Cats in scoring. The game was not without cost. The Buffaloes had long memories and a Rocky Mountain rematch was just three weeks away!

The ink on the Nebraska recruiting story had barely dried when a new controversy began to swirl. Phog Allen, speaking at the Topeka Optimist Club, alleged that a "certain Big Seven school" had illegally visited with two boys, one from Kansas City and the other from Lawrence. Allen did not divulge the school's name but did indicate that both lads attended the K-State game against Colorado. Moon Mullins, wasting little time, fired back. He agreed that it was possible that K-State had visited with the boys' parents in Lawrence and Kansas City, but not with the boys themselves. As for the lads attending the Colorado game, Mullins said "We were pleased to have as guests many prospective students at the Colorado game. The upcoming Missouri game will provide our coaches with another opportunity to have more boys as our guests. More and more young men are becoming cognizant of the fact that every man should be a Wildcat!"

Missouri (Columbia): K-State remained perfect in conference play with a narrow 55-52 win over Missouri. The Tigers, featuring a freshmen-studded team, trailed 32-26 at the half. Missouri freshman center, Bob Reiter, was unstoppable in the first half, netting 16 Tiger points. As the second half began, K-State pushed their lead to 39-28 and seemed in control. From that point on, Missouri mounted a tremendous rally and tied the game 46-46 with fewer than six minutes remaining. Knostman, Rousey, Iverson and Gibson found the range down the stretch and K-State escaped Columbia. Knostman ended the game with 21 points (and 17 rebounds) while Iverson (17) and Prisock (11) also netted double figures. Reiter paced the Tigers with 19 points.

As the Cats prepared for a quick turnaround game with Missouri, more recruiting news hit the papers. Stanley Schaetzle, one of the two boys involved in the *Omaha-Herald* recruiting story, quit school and returned to Omaha. David Bell, the other young man tied to the story, remained at K-State pending a decision from the conference.

Missouri (Manhattan): Missouri was a different team in Manhattan as K-State pounded the Tigers, 86-58. In addition to the superb Wildcat effort, the Cats also saw a school record fall. Dick Knostman scored 39 points, surpassing the previous record of 29 points set by Jack Stone (against Illinois, 1951). Knostman nailed 13 of 25 field goal attempts (and 13 of 15 from the foul line). The 39 points also tied the Big Seven record, now shared with Clyde Lovellette. Iverson and Gibson also netted double figures, as each tallied 10 points. With a conference mark of 7-0, the Cats now entered the most dangerous stretch of the season. The next four games were on the road with tests in Boulder, Lincoln, Ames and Lawrence. Gardner was very much worried about the scheduling quirk.

Colorado (Boulder): In a stunning defeat, Colorado whipped the Cats, 67-57. This was the same Colorado team that the Cats had embarrassed, 92-40. Embarrassed is the key word. The Buffs had taken exception to the Purple efforts in Manhattan. In particular, Colorado Coach H.C. Lee felt K-State continued their pressing defense late into the second half, long after the game had been decided. He had Colorado ready to play this time. "None of us could forget that game in Manhattan," said the CU skipper. "They were up by 30 points and still used a full-court press on us. That game was like our Pearl Harbor!"

The Cat players clearly took the game lightly (something Gardner readily admitted after the contest). The coach, himself, nearly missed the game. Gardner had suffered from a severe case of the flu and his trip to Boulder was a last-minute decision. The players had their own struggles, all confined to the court. Knostman managed just six points as Colorado swarmed around the Wamego junior. Iverson was equally frustrated, hitting just one fielder (in 13 attempts) as Colorado held the Cats to just 29.6% shooting (21 of 71). K-State was also badly out rebounded, 48-27. This was their worst rebounding effort in many, many games. Prisock was the only Cat in double figures, netting 17 points. The game results brought smiles all around Lawrence. The Hawks and Cats were now tied for the league lead with a showdown in Lawrence just two weeks away. Barring another upset, that game would decide the conference title!

As the Cats returned home, some additional medical news awaited them. Marion Gardner, Coach Gardner's wife, had come down with the measles. It had been a rough winter in the Gardner house. "I have seemed to come down with almost everything this year," said Gardner. "I probably will be next." As a precaution, the coach and his players all received measles shots.

Nebraska (Lincoln): K-State inched toward the showdown with KU by defeating Nebraska, 75-60. The Cornhuskers mounted a serious challenge during the opening ten minutes of the game, but the Cats then began to pull away to run their record to 8-1 in the conference (17-4 overall). The guards propelled the Purple to victory as Iverson (15) and Wilson (13) led the scoring. Fred Seger paced the Big Red with 18 points. With the win, K-State remained the number three-ranked team in the country.

As the Cats returned home, the Big Seven Conference Faculty Representatives slightly relaxed some of the recruiting rules that had been a source of controversy in the past few weeks. Big Seven coaches still would not be allowed to visit prospects off the campus during "no contact" times but could communicate with the players through telegrams and telephone conversations. Also, member institutions could not pay for traveling expenses of a prospect visiting the campus, but alums and friends of the university could pay for the trip. Gardner had earlier claimed these points had been unclear and it appeared the conference agreed with the Wildcat skipper.

Iowa State (Ames): Kansas State blitzed Iowa State, 88-66, setting a new scoring record in the process. The 88 points were the most ever scored in the Iowa State Armory by any team. Knostman scored 25 of those points, and his total also was a record for the most points ever scored by a visiting player in the Armory. The Cats jumped to an early lead and then had to withstand the ejection of Bob Rousey midway in the first half. Rousey was called for an intentional foul and was quickly sent to the showers despite the objections of Coach Gardner. As it turned out, he was hardly missed as the Wildcats zoomed to a 54-33 lead at the intermission. In addition to Knostman's 25 points, Iverson (15), Carby (11) and Prisock (10) netted double digits. KU, ranked number four in the country, was next. Both teams sported identical 9-1 records in the conference. Up for grabs was a conference title and a NCAA playoff berth. Otherwise, the game had little significance!

Kansas (Lawrence): The Kansas Jayhawks flexed their muscles and pounded K-State, 78-61. The 17-point victory hardly captured the domination of KU. Before 3,800 fans (and an estimated one million television viewers), the two teams played even until six minutes remained in the first half. Down 29-25, the Cats went ice-cold while KU hit the gas pedal. The 42-29 halftime lead was just an appetizer for KU. The Hawks shrugged off any Kansas State run in the second half and coasted to the win. K-State, which had shot nearly 38% as a team for the season, struggled against KU, hitting just 27% (20 of 74) from the field. Clyde Lovellette, in the last K-State game of his career, was magnificent, pouring in 33 points and grabbed 10 rebounds. Knostman (18) and Carby (10) paced the Cats.

After the game, Gardner was philosophical. The Hawks, in his opinion, were soon to be the kings of the NCAA playoffs. "The Big Seven is long overdue for a national champion," said the K-State coach. "If we are out of the running for the national title, I am glad Kansas will represent the conference. Phog and his boys have our very best wishes. I think they will do very well in the playoffs."

Oklahoma (Manhattan): Kansas State closed out the 1952 season with a 79-58 thrashing of Oklahoma. Fans at the game hardly watched the contest: All ears were on reports of the KU-Colorado game in Boulder. A KU loss would have forced a tie, but the Hawks secured the conference title with 72-55 win over the Buffs (Lovellette nailed 41 points). Gardner gave his four seniors ample time to shine as Iverson, Gibson, Dick Peck and Don Upson started the game along with junior Jack Carby. Iverson (22), Carby (15 points, 18 rebounds) and Gibson (10) paced the scoring. Iverson's 22 tallies pushed his season total to 309 points, the most ever scored by a K-State guard. The previous record was 298 points scored by Ernie Barrett in 1951. Iverson also was selected to play with the College All-Stars as they toured the country doing battle with the Harlem Globetrotters. He became just the second Cat (Ernie Barrett the first) to be selected to the group. Knostman ended the season with 390 points, the most ever scored in a single season by a K-State player. His average (16.3 points/game) also was a K-State single season record. Knostman was chosen to the Associated Press First Team All-Big Seven squad. The junior star from Wamego also garnered First Team All-American honors as well. Competition for the Second Team All-Big Seven squad was so close that the AP instead choose a 10-member honor roll that included Jim Iverson, Bob Rousey and Jesse Prisock as team members.

It was a disappointing end to the season for K-State. The team had clearly shown that it was the most balanced team in the conference, yet came up short at the end. Two factors hurt the Cats. First the disastrous trip to Boulder was a major blow. Second, although KU was still dominated by Lovellette, the Jayhawks began to play their best basketball in late February and early March. It was an opportune time to "get-it-together" and KU did very well in the playoffs, winning the national title by defeating St. John's University. In addition, seven Jayhawks played on the '52 Olympic Team that defeated Russia for the gold medal in Helsinki. The assistant coach of that squad was Phog Allen. In the final basketball polls, the Cats ended the season with a national ranking of number three (Associated Press) and number six (United Press).

Team Statistics (Newspaper box scores):

K-State:	1792 points	74.7/game
Opponents:	1444 points	60.0/game

Individual Scoring Leaders (Newspaper box scores):

Dick Knostman (Wamego, Ks.)	390 points	16.3/game
Jim Iverson (Mitchell, S.D.)	309 points	12.9/game
Jesse Prisock (Emporia, Ks.)	214 points	8.9/game
Jack Carby (Kansas City, Mo.)	197 points	8.6/game
Bob Rousey (Anderson, Ind.)	170 points	7.7/game
Gene Wilson (Anderson, Ind.)	139 points	5.8/game
John Gibson (Pittsburg, Ks.)	117 points	4.9/game
Dick Peck (Anderson, Ind.)	84 points	3.5/game
Don Upson (Arkansas City, Ks.)	80 points	3.3/game
Jim Smith (Brainerd, Mn.)	45 points	2.4/game
Gene Stauffer (Salina, Ks.)	27 points	1.8/game
Dan Schuyler (Anderson, Ind.)	11 points	0.8/game
Others	9 points	

NCAA CHAMPION: Kansas (28-3)
RUNNER-UP: St. Johns (New York)
THIRD PLACE: Illinois
FOURTH PLACE: Santa Clara

1953

Full Moon Over Manhattan

Record: 17-4
Conference Record: 9-3 (2nd)
Final National Ranking: 9th (UPI) & 12th (AP)
Team Captain: Dick Knostman

Kansas State Varsity Squad - top row: Roger L. Craft, Jack R. Carby, Jerry W. Jung, Gary D. Bergen, Dick W. Knostman, Jesse W. Prisock. Second row: Coach Jack Gardner, Nugent R. Adams, Walter E. Wolf, Jim A. Smith, Jim H. Tangeman, Gregg Williams, student manager, Keith "Dobbie" Lambert, assistant coach. Bottom row: Bob Rousey, Bob DeNoon, Marvin P. Mills, Gene A. Stauffer, Bill Kohl, Bob E. Smith, and Laurence "Porky" Morgan, trainer.
— Courtesy of Kansas State University Archives

As the 1953 season began, Kansas State found itself in unfamiliar surroundings. The team returned five lettermen, the fewest number of returning varsity members in the postwar era. Jack Carby, Dick Knostman, Gene Stauffer, Bob Rousey and Jesse Prisock were the returning veterans, with Knostman a First Team All-American selection (and First Team Big Seven choice) in 1952. The returning group was impressive but it would be very hard to replace Jim Iverson, Don Upson, Gene Wilson, Dick Peck and John "Hoot" Gibson. These players had helped the Cats average a school-record 74.7 points/game in 1952. In early season practices, the loss of Iverson was paramount on the mind of Gardner. The slick guard from Mitchell, South Dakota was the total package in '52. He could score from the farthest reaches of the court, was a player who possessed great desire and hustle, and set the offense in motion with deadly passing accuracy and floor leadership. The graduation of "Ivy Jim" was coupled with a second blow to K-State's back court: speedy guard Gene "The Jet" Wilson was lost to the team as well. Wilson, who had averaged 5.8 points/game as a sophomore, was drafted into the military. Gardner had to find someone to replace these two stalwarts. Early polls suggested that the experts felt Gardner would find such a player. They picked the Cats as the preseason choice to win the Big Seven.

At the same time, K-State was fielding its tallest team in the postwar era. Of the 18 players on the squad, 13 were sophomores and six of those sophomores were taller than 6'4". Jerry Jung, a sophomore from Hutchinson, was the tallest. Jung stood 6'10" tall, while fellow sophomore Gary Bergen of Independence, Missouri, stood 6'8" inches tall. Roger Craft (Garden City) tipped the measuring stick at 6'7" while Nugent Adams (Kansas City, Missouri), Walter Wolf (Norton) and Jim Smith (Brainerd, Minnesota) all were over 6'4" tall. The squad figured to be a work in progress in the early stages of the season, but with Knostman as the focus of the offense, the Cats expected to learn and win quite quickly.

On the national front, the basketball scandal was finally beginning to wind down, but not without one more bombshell. The University of Kentucky was the first to be called on the carpet. Kentucky had already been stained by the college-betting scandal. Several of its players had become legally entangled in the mess that permeated the basketball community. Bill Spivey, the All-American center who scored 22 points in the '51 championship game against K-State, was one very prominent Kentuckian to be accused. At his request, Spivey was suspended by the school until he could clear his name. The big center was charged with perjury in his testimony before a grand jury. Ultimately, after a year-long legal hassle, Spivey was exonerated of that charge and was cleared of all legal allegations, but was banned from playing in the NBA by the professional league. He sued the NBA and later settled out of court.

Coach Adolph Rupp would see his Kentucky Wildcats take a major hit. The NCAA issued its report and placed the Kentucky Wildcats on probation, canceling the entire 1953 season! In particular, the NCAA found that Kentucky had violated two specific rules, dating back to the 1947-1950 seasons. First, Kentucky acknowledged that some of its "outstanding" players received a grand total of $50,000 from sports enthusiasts, a direct violation of NCAA rules. Second, Kentucky had knowingly certified some of its athletes as eligible when the coaches were aware that these athletes were ineligible. The NCAA also charged Bradley University with the same two counts, but found that Bradley had not knowingly certified ineligible athletes.

In addition, the NCAA felt Bradley "took immediate action to correct and improve athletic practices at the school." With that in mind, the NCAA suspended Bradley from the post-season tournament but did allow them to play basketball during the 1952-53 school term. Bradley accepted their fate but Kentucky felt that its penalties were "unduly harsh and far more severe than any penalty upheld by the NCAA on any other member institution."

Jack Gardner and Phog Allen had different reactions to the news. Gardner felt the probation was "overdue," but wistfully noted that the NCAA machinery took much too long to function. Phog Allen, when asked to comment about the Kentucky probation, chose instead to make "no comment." Allen had coached Adolph Rupp at KU in the early 1920's and had great respect and admiration for his former player. Rupp was a reserve guard on the 1923 Jayhawks' team, a squad designated by the Helms Foundation as National Collegiate Champions. Rupp, and his fellow reserves, were dubbed "The Packing House Gang." Allen regularly inserted the group of rough and rugged players into the game to physically wear down their opponents as the starters rested. The group was a fan favorite and Rupp in particular had garnered a soft spot in Allen's heart. It was ironic, however. Allen had warned that the influence of money would be the ruination of the college game and he correctly read the tea leaves. It was unclear if he foresaw that his friend and former player would one day be caught square in the cross hairs of the scandal. All of this would finally be left behind: basketball was set to be played. In the first United Press poll of the season, Kansas State was picked number three in the country (behind Illinois and LaSalle).

Drake (Manhattan): The Cats had considerable trouble but edged Drake, 79-73 in overtime to open the 1953 season. The Bulldogs, who looked almost like midgets compared to the K-State giants, played instead like giants for nearly the entire game. The first half saw 11 lead changes (and 15 ties) as the Cats trailed 41-40 at the intermission. Drake opened its largest lead (63-58) with seven minutes to play when the Purple final asserted themselves. Key baskets by Knostman, Prisock and Carby helped K-State pull ahead, but Drake scored a bucket with just eight seconds remaining to force overtime. In the extra frame, six free throws and a Gene Stauffer basket helped secure the victory. Knostman was huge, scoring 32 points and grabbing 13 rebounds. Prisock added 12 tallies but overall, Gardner was hardly pleased (or impressed) with the Wildcats play. "We were lucky, very lucky," said Gardner. "It should be a great lesson to these guys." With games against Indiana and San Francisco looming, things had better improve and improve quickly.

Indiana (Manhattan): Before almost 13,000 fans K-State edged Indiana, 82-80. The difference in the tight game could be measured in feet: 40 feet to be precise! That was the distance of the buzzer-beating shot by Jack Carby that sent the crowd into wild delirium. The teams were evenly matched, with the game having 15 ties and an equal number of lead changes. K-State did manage a 46-44 lead at halftime (thanks to 16 first-half points by Knostman) but neither team could secure more than a four-point cushion in the second half. With 55 seconds remaining, K-State trailed 79-78 and Indiana went into a stall. The Cats were forced to foul and the Hoosiers made one charity, pushing their lead to 80-78. Gene Stauffer quickly countered from the corner and the teams were deadlocked one last time at 80-80. After an Indiana miscue, the Cats had one last chance, and with less than five seconds remaining Carby let fly from just inside the half-court line, ripping the nets as time expired. Knostman finished the game with 27 points while Marvin Mills (12) and Prisock (11) also nailed double digits. The win snapped the Cats' personal three-game losing streak to Indiana, and also boosted Kansas State's home court win streak to 23-games.

San Francisco (Manhattan): K-State had an easy time, defeating San Francisco, 81-60. Unlike the first two razor-thin games, the Cats jumped to a 38-18 lead at halftime and were not threatened. The damage was done before the intermission as K-State held the Dons to just 13.2% shooting (seven of 53) from the field. The Purple also out rebounded the visitors 65-49. Gardner cleared the bench as 13 Wildcats found the scoring column. Knostman (15), Stauffer (12) and Prisock (11) paced the K-State attack. Kansas State, now the number two team in the nation, departed Manhattan for their first road trip, traveling to East Lansing, Michigan for the annual Spartan Classic. There, the Cats would play Notre Dame (ranked seventh in the country) and then battle Michigan State one night later.

Notre Dame (East Lansing): K-State dumped the Irish from the unbeaten ranks, defeating Notre Dame 80-64 in the Spartan Classic. After some tight opening minutes, the Cats pulled away to a 44-28 halftime lead and coasted to the win. The margin of victory shocked the gathered crowd, including many East Coast sports writers and broadcasters. Knostman was his usual impressive self, netting 22 points. Prisock added 13 while Gary Bergen, a heralded sophomore from Independence, Missouri, added 10 tallies.

Michigan State (East Lansing): All of the accolades that came from the Notre Dame game quickly vanished as Michigan State pounded the Cats, 80-63. The Spartans, coached by Pete Newell, completely stopped Knostman, holding him to just one field goal. The Wamego star did nail 13 of 15 free throws, however, but Michigan State clearly had his number the entire game. The first ten minutes were closely contested as both teams took turns sharing narrow leads. The final ten minutes of the first half, however, belonged to the Spartans. Michigan State went on a 8-0 run and cruised to a 41-30 lead at the intermission. The advantage grew to 19 early in the final half and K-State fell to its first defeat. In addition to Knostman's 15 points, Bob Rousey was the only other Cat in double figures with 12 tallies. The Wildcats returned to Manhattan to regroup before leaving for Kansas City and the Holiday Tournament. Yale joined the Big Seven family in the annual gathering at Municipal Auditorium.

Oklahoma (Kansas City): The Cats opened the holiday bash in fine form by clawing Oklahoma, 93-69. K-State never trailed and scored the most points ever tallied by a Wildcat team against the Sooners. The Purple started quickly and had an early seven-point cushion before exploding for a 47-28 halftime lead. The game was decided and Gardner freely substituted in the final half. Prisock (14), Knostman (13), Carby (11) and Jim Smith (10) all netted double figures. K-State would have an unlikely second-round opponent. Yale upset a highly regarded Colorado squad, 56-54. Joining the Cats and Bulldogs in the semi-finals were KU and Missouri.

Yale (Kansas City): Kansas State defeated Yale, 79-70, and advanced to an all-Kansas final. The score was much closer than the game as the Cats opened a quick seven-point lead and then zoomed to a 37-26 advantage at the half. Yale crawled to within four points but drew no closer as Knostman (20), Stauffer (12), Prisock (11) and Carby (10) all netted double figures. It was a rather unimpressive win and Gardner was greatly incensed with the Cat's defense (or lack thereof).Yale coach Howard Hobson also was not overly impressed with the Cats. He felt that K-State was not much better than the Navy team that pounded Yale earlier in the year. Next up for the Purple was a battle with KU for the championship.

Gardner and Allen were both quite adept at lobbing verbal bombs at each other but prior to this game the two were rather quiet. Gardner praised the Hawks and simply looked forward to the challenge. When asked about K-State, one sportswriter felt Phog Allen may have set a new personal record: a record of silence! Allen said absolutely nothing to the scribe, shrugged his shoulders and walked away from the interview. It prompted several reporters to ask Assistant Coach Dick Harp if the venerable doctor was sick! He was not, but Harp felt KU was a serious underdog in the upcoming tilt.

The Wildcats proudly show the trophy they received for winning the Big Seven tournament.
— Courtesy of Kansas State University Archives

Kansas (Kansas City): Kansas State captured its third holiday tournament title with a 93-87 victory over Kansas. The Cats, now the number one team in the land, rode a 38-point performance from Knostman to gain the win. The game more closely resembled a back-alley brawl. A total of 64 fouls was whistled in the contest (33 for KU, 31 for K-State), a tournament record. The 95 free throws attempted was also a tourney record. The Cats made 35 of 48 charities while

KU netted 31 of 47 attempts. Neither team developed much offensive rhythm in the first half. With 41 fouls called, how could they? KU star B.H. Born, the slender 6'9" pivot from Medicine Lodge, fouled out with 5:29 left in the first half. Despite the officials, the Cats did manage a 48-40 lead at the intermission. The Jayhawks were hardly in awe of the Wildcats and in the second half made run after run at the victors. They never were able to seize the lead, however, and K-State grabbed the title. In addition to Knostman, Stauffer (13), Rousey (12), Jim Smith (12) and Prisock (10) netted double digits. KU was led by Allen Kelley (18) and Harold Patterson (14). Born played just 12 minutes in the game and was in constant foul trouble, managing a mere two points in the defeat.

Knostman's 38 points was just one short of the tourney record (set by Oklahoma's Sherm Norton in the 1951 tournament). With three minutes remaining in the game, Knostman came to the bench. Gardner, informed that his prize player needed just two points to break the tournament record, quickly sent the senior star back into the game. He never touched the ball again. The Jayhawks gained possession of the basketball and then stalled the final 2:30 minutes of the game! The fans booed the Hawks mercilessly for the strategy. After the contest, Phog Allen said that the move was not meant to disrespect Knostman, but rather to "get KU points." Most observers disagreed, wondering if KU was more concerned about the Cats breaking the century mark in scoring. It was a great K-State win but also a foreshadowing of the upcoming conference season. The Wildcats were not the prohibitive champion-to-be as everyone had thought. KU, hardly mentioned all season as a serious contender, demonstrated in Kansas City that they would figure into the championship mix. In the history of the Big Seven, the eventual champion many times had to successfully navigate both Manhattan and Lawrence. In 1953, things would remain true to form.

Marquette (Manhattan): Kansas State had one final non-conference game left and defeated Marquette, 88-72. This was no ordinary game however: this was the homecoming for Tex Winter, the Marquette coach. Winter, who had served as Gardner's assistant from 1947-51, was accorded a hero's return to Manhattan. The Marquette team train was met at the McFarland, Kansas, Rock Island depot by a band, Manhattan civic leaders and K-State students. From there, a caravan led the team into town where lunch was served and Winter was presented the key to

Marquette's Tex Winter confers with Coach Gardner before the game.
— Courtesy of Kansas State University Archives

the city by Manhattan Mayor Richard Rogers. The event was planned by Coach Gardner and Lud Fiser, manager of the Manhattan Chamber of Commerce. Winter had been instrumental in recruiting many of the current Cat players and Knostman, in particular, credited Winter with teaching him the hook shot, which the Wildcat All-American had used so effectively. In the midst of all of the festivities, there was a game to play. The first half was a tight affair as K-State's Bob Rousey put together the beginnings of a career night. Rousey netted 17 points in the first half as K-State held a slim 47-43 lead at the intermission. The Hilltoppers cut that lead to just two points early in the second half before the Cats steadily pulled away for the win. Rousey ended the contest with 22 points, a career high for the guard from Anderson, Indiana. Knostman led all scorers with 26 points while Prisock added 13. K-State improved its record to 8-1 and was the number one-ranked team in the country. Despite the win, Gardner was concerned. Marquette was a young team and the coach felt the Cats defense was far too "generous" to the young visitors. Also, the Hilltoppers won the battle of the boards. Both issues were red flags as the Cats prepared for KU.

Kansas (Lawrence): In a shocking upset, KU manhandled the Wildcats, 80-66, in Lawrence. The red flags that had appeared in the Marquette game were in full view to the nearly 4,000 fans who jammed Hoch Auditorium. The Hawks totally dominated the Cats. KU out rebounded the Wildcats and held the Purple to 28.6% shooting from the field (18 of 63). It was the Cats' worst shooting effort of the year. B.H. Born, the KU center, poured in 31 points (and swiped 20 rebounds) to lead all scorers while Rousey (16) paced the Wildcats. Jim Smith added 12 while Knostman, who was battered around the entire night, managed 12 tallies on just four-of-20 shooting from the field. Knostman's point total was significant. With the 12 points, he became the all-time leading scorer at Kansas State (827 points) surpassing Rick Harman (820 points). Knostman's point total was achieved in just over two full seasons of play (Harman's in four full seasons). The Wamego senior no doubt would have traded the record for a Cat win. After the game, both coaches commented about the upcoming game in Manhattan. Gardner made a rather cryptic remark when he said "Tonight we had no one who could stop Born, but we will the next time!" For his part, Allen turned scriptural. "The Lord giveth and the Lord taketh away," said the head Jayhawk. "When we go to Manhattan, Jack's boys are going to run all over us. K-State will easily win the conference." Sport writers wondered out loud: had Phog suddenly turned into Jack Gardner's biggest fan or was this more of Allen's reverse psychology? They would get their answer in exactly 30 days!

Missouri (Columbia): In a record-shattering night, K-State rebounded from the KU defeat and edged Missouri, 94-85. The Cats raced to a 37-25 lead at the half and pushed the margin to 18 points when Gardner rested the starters. The Tigers capitalized and cut the lead to just five (80-75), even after Gardner had re-inserted the regulars. Knostman, who ended the game with 23 points, added four crucial buckets in the final four minutes to stamp out the Missouri fire. Stauffer and Rousey added 15 points each while Marvin Mills nailed 10. The Tigers were paced in scoring by Bob Reiter, who popped in 27 points. Records fell during the game. The 94 points scored were the most ever scored by a K-State team against Missouri, and the most points ever scored by any opponent in Brewer Field House. Offense was hardly the problem. Defense was. The 85 points were the most Missouri had scored all season, and the most the Tigers ever scored against K-State. Few teams had ever claimed a conference title with such a porous defense.

Either K-State tightened the defensive screws or they would have to take their chances with a potent offense.

As the Cats prepared for Iowa State, more news was being made at the student hospital. Bob Rousey had sustained a serious foot injury at Missouri and was on crutches. He would miss the bout against the Cyclones. Knostman was battling the flu while Carby was nursing a deep leg bruise. Both were questionable for the game against Iowa State. For the media, the most sought-after Wildcat was not Coach Gardner or his players. Everyone wanted to chat with K-State trainer, Lawrence "Porky" Morgan.

Iowa State (Manhattan): Iowa State nearly ended any Kansas State chances of a conference title, but the Cats held on, defeating the Cyclones 81-78. The visitors from Ames were hardly expected to even challenge the Wildcats but the game was tight the entire night. K-State led 40-38 at the half and as the 12,000 fans watched in horror, the Cyclones battled the Purple blow-for-blow in the second half as well. K-State finally inched away in the last three minutes to claim their 10th win in 12 starts. Rousey was unable to play due to the ankle injury sustained at Missouri and Carby was available only for limited minutes. Knostman, however, showed little effects of the flu bug. The Wamego native poured in 21 points, but he was not the leading K-State scorer. That honor went to Gene Stauffer. In the best game of his career, the Salina junior scored 24 points. Gary Bergen added 13 in his finest effort as well. Iowa State was led by their 6'8" star Delmar Diercks, who poured in 26 points.

Nebraska (Lincoln): In a stunning defeat, Nebraska upended the Cats, 80-67. K-State had one early lead (7-5) but the game belonged totally to the Cornhuskers. Down 44-36 at the half, the Cats made one run in the second half and cut the lead to two, 47-45. There would be no other challenges as Knostman (21), Stauffer (17) and Jim Smith (11) netted double figures. The loss was a critical blow to the Cats. With a conference record of 2-2, the Wildcats could not afford another conference loss, and if that occurred, they then would need some luck from other teams if they were to claim the top spot in the Big Seven.

Iowa State (Ames): K-State defeated an energized Cyclone squad, 74-64, to gain their third conference win. The Cats seemed in control, leading 38-26 at the intermission. Iowa State quickly trimmed that deficit to just two points before Knostman rallied the Purple with several buckets to give K-State somewhat of a cushion. The Cyclones were not done, however, and tied the game 55-55 before the visitors pulled away. Knostman ended the game with 31 points, a record performance in the Iowa State Armory. Stauffer added 10. Delmar Diercks paced the Cyclones with 20 points. The win was Gardner's 283rd victory in his career, and the 141st victory while coaching in Manhattan. That K-State total (achieved in less than 10 seasons) was nearly one-half of the 286 wins that the school had recorded in the 35 seasons of basketball prior to Gardner's arrival at Kansas State! With five of the remaining seven conference games in Manhattan (including a showdown with KU), the Cats still had a good chance to win the conference. What they needed was to play solid defense, rebound and avoid any distractions as they came down the stretch run. Distractions were just what they got.

On February 10th (one day after the Iowa State game), Gardner was named the coach of the College All-Star's team. At the end of each season, a chosen squad of college seniors would travel around the country, playing games against the Harlem Globetrotters. At first blush, it seemed like an honor for the Wildcat skipper. Former K-State players Ernie Barrett and Jim Iverson had played for the All-Stars in recent years and there seemed to be little concern about Gardner accepting the coaching position. But there was concern, big concern, and it started in the office of Wildcat Athletics Director Moon Mullins. Mullins refused to give Gardner permission to coach the team. In 1952, Jim Iverson had accepted a roster spot and played with the All-Stars. By playing in the games (for pay), Iverson forfeited his eligibility to play baseball for the Cats (and he was a fine pitcher, the best on the squad). At the time, Mullins was not pleased. "Something is wrong when an athlete places the tour and the money he will receive over school spirit and responsibility," said Mullins. With Gardner, Mullins was clear. There were no hidden motives, just a sincere desire to keep Kansas State far removed from mingling with the pros. "I think colleges are making a mistake in going along with this sort of thing," said Mullins. "Don't get me wrong. I like professional sports and I like the Globetrotters. But there is a place for college sports and there is a place for professional sports. I don't think the two should mix."

Most basketball fans (and Gardner himself) were surprised by the announcement. Coaches had routinely accepted these coaching positions in the off-season. Oklahoma football great Bud Wilkinson had coached the College Football All-Stars as they played members of the National Football League. Phog Allen himself had worked on an All-Star basketball bench against the Globetrotters in 1951. If Gardner was upset, he wasn't talking, and neither was Kansas State President James McCain or Athletic Council President, Eric Tebow. Ringside observers, however, had sensed a simmering feud between Mullins and Gardner brewing, and now felt Mullins had decided to force a showdown. As the story went, if the athletic director did not have the full support of the K-State brass (and with that, full authority in his office), he would walk. Mullins denied the "showdown" talk as just speculation. There was another story, however, that Mullins also had become upset with a downtown Manhattan alumni group which helped in the recruitment of players. Most insiders surmised that Gardner used the alumni group to bypass Mullins in certain instances. The entire affair was messy, now more so since it became public. Gardner appeared to have three distinct choices: he could defy Mullins and accept the position; he could appeal the decision to the athletic council or to President McCain himself, or he could forget the whole thing. Most observers felt the last choice was highly unlikely. With the next athletic council meeting scheduled to take place in several weeks, a decision was expected.

As everyone at K-State grew silent, Phog Allen grew talkative. On a radio show from Lawrence, Allen announced he had twice turned down the same coaching position. "This year I was offered $3,000," said Allen, "and when I turned them down again, they told me I could write my own ticket."

"I never even considered making the trip," continued Allen. "It's strictly a professional proposition and I don't think it would reflect well on the college if I went on a professional tour."

Allen indicated that each player usually received between $1,000-$1,500 for the trip. The KU mentor had coached in several All-Star games but they were for charity. "Even in those games I always was certain to get permission from Arthur Lonborg, our athletic director," concluded

Allen. "I'd never do anything without his consent." Many sports writers felt the final comments were a backhanded slap at Gardner.

Allen's comments were not supported, however. Both Irving Marsh, the Assistant Sports Editor of the *New York Tribune Herald* and Abe Saperstein, the owner of the Globetrotters, were mentioned as men who could confirm Allen's recollections. When asked to comment, they had quite different accounts. Both felt Allen at best "misunderstood" their overtures. Allen was asked to serve as a ceremonial coach when the Trotters visited Kansas City, but both men were equally certain that Allen had never been offered the coaching position for the entire tour. K-State fans were all to familiar with Allen's verbal tactics but frankly this time they were too concerned to care. The Mullins-Gardner feud was very serious and as each day passed without any official comment, the Kansas State faithful grew more worried by the minute!

Knostman broke Lovellette's record by hitting 42.
— Courtesy of Kansas State University Archives

Oklahoma (Manhattan): In the midst of all the media frenzy, K-State had a game to play and they played quite well, pounding Oklahoma 84-64. The Cat team scored exactly one-half of the points. Dick Knostman scored the other half! The Wamego senior poured in a Big Seven record 42 points, bettering the 41 points scored by KU's Clyde Lovellette (against Colorado) during the 1952 season. Knostman also set a Kansas State record when he snared 23 rebounds, surpassing his own previous record of 22 rebounds grabbed against Iowa State in 1952. Bergen (15) and Rousey (12) also nailed double figures. The introduction of Gardner prior to the game was an event in itself. The coach received a thunderous ovation that lasted nearly 30 seconds. The talk before the game concerned a letter written by Manhattan backers of Gardner. The letter was sent to K-State alumni, encouraging them to write or call President McCain in support of the coach. From all appearances, the letter was having the desired effect.

With a conference record of 4-2, the Cats prepared to battle the 6-2 KU Jayhawks in Manhattan. A K-State win would send the Cats back into the conference title picture. A loss would all but end their chances for the title and post-season play. The game would also be the "rubber match" between Gardner and Allen: in the previous 24 encounters, each coach had won 12 games.

Kansas (Manhattan): KU delivered a fatal blow to K-State, defeating the Cats 80-78. The Hawks led for most of the game and held a 79-76 lead with less than a minute to play. The

Cats' Gary Bergen nailed a tip-in with 45 seconds remaining and when KU tried to stall, the Purple forced a turnover. With K-State down by one point, the Jayhawks' Ken Buller fouled the Wildcats' Bob Smith with just 10 seconds remaining. Kansas State fans were in hysterics as the sophomore from Hope, Kansas, went to the line. Smith missed the first free throw and then missed the second. The Hawks secured the rebound and scored a final point as KU's Dean Smith was fouled in the rebounding scramble. The loss snapped the Wildcats' home-court winning streak at 28 games and gave K-State a record of 4-3 in the conference. Knostman (27), Prisock (13) and Bergen (11) led the Cats while B.H. Born nailed 27 to pace the Hawks. KU improved their record to 7-2 and grabbed control of the conference lead.

The Mullins-Gardner issue continued to bubble. On February 19th, (two days after the KU game), the K-State Athletic Council met. No one from the group would speak publicly but it was widely speculated that, if forced into a corner, the K-State brass would back Mullins. It was unclear exactly what happened in the meeting. The media was rampant with many possible scenarios. Whatever transpired, on February 20th Gardner withdrew his name from the Globetrotter coaching position.

In a prepared statement, Gardner said "When I accepted the invitation to serve as coach, to my knowledge there had never been any interpretation of Big Seven or NCAA rules that would prevent my participation in this or similar events where professionals were involved. In 1951, Phog Allen served as a honorary coach on the tour stop in Kansas City, and I did the same in 1952. Many coaches across the country have taken part in this or similar events. However, with the best interests of Kansas State in mind, I have asked the Globetrotters to relieve me from the coaching responsibilities."

Eric Tebow, Chairman of the Kansas State Athletic Council, tried to put a cap on the developments with four short words: "This closes the matter." He could only wish! Several newspapers reported that Gardner had attended the athletic council meeting and pleaded his case, hoping for a reversal of Mullins' decision. The sources also indicated that by a vote of 8-1, Gardner was rejected but was allowed to save face by resigning from the coaching position. It was also hoped that this move would placate the many Gardner supporters who were growing quite weary of Mullins. As it turned out, it wouldn't be quite that neat and tidy. The final bits of dust and dirt from this mess would finally be swept up in a few short months.

Colorado (Boulder): K-State kept its slim conference championship hopes alive with a 81-56 pounding of Colorado. The Buffaloes enjoyed one lead (16-15) early in the game before the Cats pulled away with surprising ease. Rousey (19), Knostman (12) and Bergen (11) notched double figures. The win was a measure of revenge. Colorado had defeated the Wildcats in Boulder in 1952, a loss that devastated the Cats' conference title chances. Knostman quietly also made some news: with his 12 points, he became the first Wildcat to score over 1000 points in his career.

Missouri (Manhattan): The Wildcats defeated Missouri, 75-68, to improve their conference record to 6-3. The Tigers were a stubborn bunch who twice in the second half cut 15-point deficits to just four points. They drew no closer as Knostman (18), Stauffer (15) and Prisock (15) scored in double digits. Prisock provided a big offensive boost. He had lost his starting position but ably came off the bench. His four points late in the game extinguished the last Missouri rally and helped preserve the victory. The Cats' prospects for a conference title were simple. With three games remaining, K-State had to "win-out" and hope someone could upset the 7-2 KU Jayhawks. If that took place, the Cats could at least secure a tie for the conference top spot.

Colorado (Manhattan): Kansas State clung to diminishing conference title hopes, defeating Colorado 88-69. The Buffaloes battled the Wildcats on even terms, and trailed 67-65 with just six minutes to play. K-State then held the visitors scoreless for more than four minutes while scoring 14 points of their own. The result was a lopsided victory, but one that was hardly convincing. Rousey (22), Knostman (18) and Stauffer (10) led the efforts. Five Buffs scored in double figures, including Colorado's sensational sophomore, Art Bunte. His story would become front page news for Wildcat fans in the summer months to come! Two nights later, the Buffaloes lost to KU, as the Jayhawks remained in the driver's seat for the conference championship. B.H. Born netted 44 points, besting the previous record (42) set by Knostman just three weeks earlier.

As the season wound down, honors for Knostman began to pour in. He was chosen to the Second Team All-Star squad by *Collier's Magazine*, and was named a Second Team All-American by the Associated Press. Knostman was also named a Second Team All-American by the United Press, and was a First Team All-American by the Newspaper Enterprises Association (NEA). *Look Magazine* and the Helms Foundation also selected the Wamego senior to their First Team All-American squad.

The city of Manhattan was also in the national spotlight. K-State would be hosting the Western Regional Playoffs and the entire city was busy trying to assure that all of the fans, coaches, teams and media had accommodations. Manhattan had only two hotels at the time (The Wareham and The Gillett) and many Manhattan residents were renting out their rooms (and homes) to the swarm of basketball followers that soon would be descending on the town. K-State fans could only hope for a miracle that the Cats would be one of the four teams that played in Manhattan.

Oklahoma (Norman): In their last road game of the year, the Cats flattened Oklahoma, 76-60. K-State led the entire game and had perhaps the most balanced scoring effort of the entire season. Five Wildcats scored in double figures: Prisock (15), Rousey (15), Knostman (14), Jim Smith (13) and Bergen (12). K-State's chances for any conference title ended, however, as KU defeated Missouri. It was the second straight conference title for the Jayhawks but unlike the 1952 crown, this one was totally unexpected. K-State had been an overwhelming choice to win the title while KU had hardly garnered even a whisper of attention as the season began. The Hawks had beaten K-State twice during the regular season and now added one more measure of indignity to cap the year. When asked about the upcoming regional games in Manhattan, Phog Allen was exuberant. "K-State was such a huge favorite to win the conference," beamed the KU boss. "Now they are going to serve as ushers for us in the NCAA playoffs!" All of this left a bitter taste in the mouths of Wildcat fans. Was it possible to feel any lower? The answer would be forthcoming in just a few weeks!

Nebraska (Manhattan): K-State closed out the '53 season with a resounding 108-80 blistering of Nebraska. The point total was a conference record, surpassing the 99-point performance by the Cats against Iowa State in Nichols Gymnasium in 1950. The game was the final curtain call for seniors Knostman, Rousey and Carby. Knostman ended the game with 28 points while Rousey (15) and Carby (11) joined their classmate in scoring double figures. Prisock also netted double digits, hitting for 21 points. The win also avenged the Cats' crippling 80-67 loss to the Cornhuskers in Lincoln. KU would advance to the national championship game, where the Hawks were edged by Indiana, 69-68.

With the season concluded, post-season honors continued for several Wildcats. Knostman was chosen as a First Team All Conference selection (both UP and AP) while Rousey was a Second Team choice by both newspapers. In addition, Stauffer and Bergen grabbed Honorable Mention selections by the Associated Press. Rousey and Knostman were chosen to play in the Arafat Shrine East-West All-Star game (in Kansas City) and would be coached by Jack Gardner. The West squad, guided by Gardner, defeated the East squad, 91-77, as Rousey (26) and Knostman (19) paced the victors. Knostman and Rousey also joined the College All-Star tour as they battled the Harlem Globetrotters in games played across the country. Gardner, who had been selected to coach the all-stars before he was forced to resign the post, was replaced by DePaul Coach Ray Meyer and Seton Hall Coach Honey Russell. The final scene of the "Globetrotter mess" would soon be acted out.

Team Statistics (Newspaper box scores):

Kansas State:	1710 points	81.4/game
Opponents:	1519 points	72.3/game

Individual Scoring Leaders (Newspaper box scores):

Dick Knostman (Wamego, Ks.)	476 points	22.7/game
Bob Rousey (Anderson, Ind.)	215 points	10.8/game
Gene Stauffer (Salina, Ks.)	211 points	10.5/game
Jess Prisock (Emporia, Ks.)	207 points	9.9/game
Jim Smith (Brainerd, Minn.)	159 points	7.6/game
Gary Bergen (Independence, Mo.)	146 points	7.0/game
Marvin Mills (Tulsa, Ok.)	104 points	5.0/game
Jack Carby (Kansas City, Mo.)	103 points	4.9/game
Jerry Jung (Hutchinson, Ks.)	44 points	2.3/game
Nugent Adams (Kansas City, Mo.)	19 points	1.3/game
Bob Smith (Hope, Ks.)	12 points	1.3/game
Others	14 points	

NCAA CHAMPION: Indiana (23-3)
RUNNER-UP: Kansas
THIRD PLACE: Washington
FOURTH PLACE: LSU

1954
Heading West

As the spring days grew longer in Manhattan, everything appeared normal at K-State. Gardner was busy speaking on the "mashed-potato circuit," addressing various civic and school groups across the state. As the school days wound down, Gardner even conducted spring drills, preparing the basketball squad for the 1954 season. A normal, hot Manhattan summer seemed just around the corner. It wouldn't remain normal, but certainly would be hot!

Hints of a change surfaced on June 9. Several newspapers confirmed that Gardner was a leading candidate for the head coaching job at the University of Utah. The story was incorrect. Gardner was not A candidate. Gardner was THE candidate to replace Utah coach Vadal Peterson, who had coached the Utes for 26 seasons. The Utah school had considered 37 coaches and Gardner was the clear choice of the Utah Board of Regents. It was up to the K-State coach, and on June 10 Gardner formally announced his decision. On that day, Gardner first attended a lengthy meeting with President James McCain and Dean R.I. Throckmorton, the newly appointed Chairman of the K-State Athletic Council. When the meeting adjourned, Gardner phoned Utah with his acceptance of the Ute coaching position. In a formal statement, Gardner said he was leaving Manhattan with "much regret," but was anxious for his new duties at the Salt Lake City campus. "I will miss the fine players and many friends that we have here in Manhattan," said Gardner. "I know I am entering into another tough league and look forward to the challenges ahead."

Kansas State was caught off-guard by the developments. President McCain hurriedly issued a statement expressing regret, but assured K-Staters that "every reasonable effort was made to persuade Gardner that it would be in his best interests to stay in Manhattan." McCain also promised swift action by the Kansas State Athletic Council to find a suitable replacement.

Athletic Director Moon Mullins, informed of Gardner's announcement, said "I hope Jack is as happy in his new tour of duty as he has been at Kansas State." Mullins made no other statements. Gardner's new salary would be $9,500/year, just $60 more than his Kansas State salary.

K-State fans were in a tizzy! At first blush, the rift between Mullins and Gardner seemed to be the only reason for the coach to leave Manhattan. The Utah field house could hardly compare to K-State's palace (the Utes played in a building that seated 6,000 fans) and the difference in money was almost insignificant. In addition, the Cats played in the very prestigious Big Seven Conference while Utah was a member of the Skyline Conference. It was a fine conference but hardly comparable to the Big Seven. To Gardner loyalists, the evidence seemed quite conclusive: the feud between the two men had to be the reason Gardner left K-State.

The feud was just one reason Gardner left, however. The Utah school frankly offered Gardner many basketball opportunities that the Big Seven (and Kansas State) could not. The Skyline Conference was not as restrictive as the Big Seven. Schools from that conference were encouraged to play tough non-conference games anywhere at any time. Teams regularly made West and East Coast trips to play the heavyweights. The league also did not frown on its teams playing in the National Invitational Tournament, something the Big Seven Conference refused to allow. The NIT ban was one major gripe that had displeased Gardner while at K-State. The Skyline Conference also had not rushed to adopt the tough regulations that restricted coaches from talking with prospective students. Many conferences adopted these policies and the Big Seven Faculty Representatives, not to be left out, had eagerly embraced them as well, perhaps not fully aware of the consequences. Utah and the other Skyline member schools had been more thoughtful. They waited until the NCAA made its recommendations before implementing any regulations.

K-State wasted little time in finding Gardner's replacement. On June 18, Kansas State announced that Fred "Tex" Winter would become the 14th coach at the college. Winter had served as Gardner's assistant coach from 1947 to 1951 before he took over the head job at Marquette University, where he had coached the past two seasons. The choice of Winter was a natural. Whether by coincidence or not, Kansas State had enjoyed its greatest success during the four seasons that Winter assisted Gardner. During that time, the Cats won two conference titles outright, tied for a third title and advanced to the Final Four two times. Winter's arrival served as a huge cushion for the jolt K-State fans felt with Gardner's departure.

After a trip to Salt Lake City, Gardner returned to Manhattan and spent the summer of 1953 preparing his family for the move west. As the summer turned into early September, K-State was to feel the next blow from the Gardner move. On September 6, newspapers reported that Wildcat junior Gary Bergen was considering a transfer to Utah to join Gardner. Bergen had traveled to Boulder, Colorado, where he visited with CU star, Art Bunte. Both, it seemed, were now considering a move to Salt Lake City! Winter visited with the Wildcat star and reported that Bergen was only vacationing in Boulder and would return to Manhattan to enroll for the fall semester. "I visited with Gary and he assured me that he was returning to K-State," said the new Wildcat boss. "Until I hear otherwise, I have faith that he'll keep his word." Bergen changed his mind, however, and notified Winter and K-State (by letter) that he was heading to Utah. Bunte joined him at the Salt Lake City campus. Gardner was elated at the prospects. "Any coach would be pleased to have such fine athletes playing for him," said Gardner. "I am no exception."

Tex Winter, Moon Mullins and President McCain were angered by the move and Gardner's recruitment of Bergen. "I am very disappointed in the tactics that Jack has used to negotiate this transfer," said Winter. "Bergen's transfer to Utah is both unethical and unorthodox. Jack had assured me that he didn't plan to work on any of the boys. I wonder if there are any ethics left in college athletics. I wonder, too, at Jack's ethics when he would deal with me in such a manner." Gardner was hardly fazed, and noted that players transferred all the time when coaches moved to new positions. This appeared to be more than that, however. Newspapers reported that Bergen was "coached" by Gardner to deceive Kansas State. The Wildcat star was told to tell K-State that he planned on returning to Manhattan, and then at the last moment, make his move to Utah. Whatever the strategy, the result was the same: Bergen was gone and so was sophomore Ted Berner, who had played on the junior varsity for the Cats in the 1953 season.

Kansas newspapers wasted little time in blasting Gardner. Many sportswriters half-jokingly implored K-State to firmly secure the field house itself or Gardner might just move it to Salt Lake as well! Newspapers also reported that Wildcat Jerry Jung received a letter from the Salt Lake City school encouraging him to "visit the Utah campus." Jung, unlike Bergen and Berner, stayed in Manhattan.

While the media criticized Gardner at nearly every turn, K-State fans were hardly unanimous in their condemnation of Gardner. Many felt the school administration had needlessly pushed him into a corner, and now were getting some payback.

The Bergen controversy would not be officially over without a word from Phog Allen. The media was drooling at the prospect of the venerable KU coach commenting on the sideshow in Manhattan. Allen delivered! "They are celebrating frontier days out in Oregon, Washington and Utah," said the KU skipper, "with the old-timers wearing beards to commemorate the event. It will not be surprising if Grandpa Brannum, Lew Hitch, Harold Howey and the itinerant Jack Carby show up on the Utah campus, grow beards and begin playing basketball for their old coach Jack Gardner!"

Tex Winter was unfortunately swept into the Purple swirl. Without Bergen, Winter's 1954 team posted a record of 11-10 (5-7 in the conference) and tied for fourth in the Big Seven. His 1955 team improved to a record of 11-10 overall (6-6 in the conference) and a third place finish in the Big Seven. After these two seasons, Tex made his own mark. Winter's teams would win or tie for eight conference titles, qualify for two Final Four appearances and win 262 games in 15 seasons in Manhattan. Only Jack Hartman would win more games as a K-State coach. In later years, Winter also collected nine NBA Championship rings as a coach for the Chicago Bulls and Los Angeles Lakers. Not bad for a coach who endured signs and banners in 1954 that read "Spring is Here, Winter Must Go!"

As Winter gradually won over the Kansas State campus, some of the adulation for Gardner began to fade. In the spring of 1954, the NCAA placed K-State on one year's probation for violations of the athletic code. The Wildcats were cited for staging "tryouts" for perspective athletes and also were singled out because of the existence of an organization in Manhattan known as the Wildcat Club. It was this very club that had irritated Moon Mullins. The investigation found that K-State was lax in the administration and conduct of its athletic affairs, particularly with the Wildcat Club. "The Club collected funds in the amount of at least $59,500 for use in part to defray out-of-state travel and entertainment costs for K-State's basketball and football staff members," reported the NCAA. "This money was also used to finance certain athletic department functions. There existed no complete and accurate accounting of these disbursements." The findings were serious but the NCAA was quick to report that the funds collected by the Wildcat Club did not personally benefit any athletes. The infractions, dating back as far as 1947, would not preclude the Wildcats from any post-season basketball competition in 1955. The NCAA and the Big Seven Faculty Representatives did publicly commend K-State Athletic Director Moon Mullins and President James McCain for taking major steps to ensure that future violations would not take place.

Gardner received his own admonishment in the spring of 1955. The Utah coach was verbally blistered by the NCAA for obtaining players by methods they termed both "unsportsmanlike and unethical." The council found that in 1953 Gardner had "resorted to deception, and encouraged deception, by advising Gary Bergen, Jerry Jung and Roger Craft to collaborate in not revealing to Kansas State officials that they were planning to transfer from K-State to Utah." Jung and Craft remained at K-State while Bergen left for Salt Lake City. No fault was found with either the University of Utah or Kansas State in the matter.

Gardner's stay at Utah was long and successful. With both Bunte and Bergen having to sit out the 1954 season, Utah struggled to an 12-14 record. Once the two transfers became eligible, the Utes became good very quickly. The '55 team posted a 24-4 record with Bunte the leading scorer (averaging 19.2 points/game) while Bergen was the leading rebounder (12.8 caroms/game). The '56 team went 22-6, with Bunte again the scoring leader (22.6 points/game) while Bergen grabbed 12.0 rebounds/game. Even today, Bunte is the 24th leading scorer in Utah history. He also was an All-American at the Utah school. Both teams won conference titles and advanced to the NCAA Tournament where they lost in the first round. It was just a start for Gardner. In 18 seasons, Gardner's teams won 339 games (losing 154) for a winning percentage of 68.8%. Only Vadal Peterson, who had a record of 385-230 in 26 seasons, had won more games for the Utes. Gardner's teams won or tied for seven Skyline Conference Titles. He also took two Utah teams to the Final Four, placing fourth in both the 1961 and 1966 seasons. Gardner became the first (and only) coach in NCAA history to take two different schools to the Final Four two times. Just as at Kansas State, Gardner's teams also inspired a building project on the Salt Lake City campus. In 1969, Utah completed the 15,000 seat Special Events Center (later renamed the Jon M. Huntsman Center). The enormous reflective dome, the largest in the world, is an unmistakable landmark on the campus. Gardner also was named National Coach of the Year in 1970. The Utah mentor, nicknamed the "Silver Fox," also received no fewer than 10 different Hall of Fame nominations, including one at Kansas State. Gardner retired from the Utes head position in 1971. In later years, he served as a consultant for the NBA Utah Jazz and is credited with persuading the Jazz to draft future NBA legend John Stockton. All told, in 28 seasons of coaching at the major college level, Gardner won 486 games and lost 235. He passed away on April 9, 2000, in Salt Lake City.

Jack Gardner. Although his coaching career began in southern California and ended in Utah, his resume of accomplishments drips with the color purple. In 1939, a young man settled in Manhattan, Kansas, with confidence and tenacity that few could match. His hard work and dedication put Kansas State basketball on the map, not just in Kansas, but across the nation. His enthusiasm, coupled with the perseverance of some very dedicated K-State administrators, literally built the field house, which later would be named Ahearn Field House. Mike Ahearn had long envisioned a big arena, but Gardner's exciting teams fueled a frenzy to build. The field house, rightly named for Ahearn, sometimes affectionately was called "The House that Jack Built." As a coach, Gardner raised the bar of what Kansas State basketball could (and should) be. Although his final days in Manhattan were clouded in controversy, his legacy is found in the teams he coached and the memories they created. Coaches like Tex Winter, Cotton Fitzsimmons, Jack Hartman, Lon Kruger, Dana Altman, Tom Asbury, Jim Wooldridge and Bob Huggins have attempted to raise the bar to newer heights. Some were successful while others were not. At the writing of this book, the Cats have turned to Frank Martin as their new coach. History will judge Coach Martin, as it has with the others before him. All of these coaches, no matter their legacy at Kansas State, share a commonality of great distinction: They followed Jack Gardner. It's Time to Play!

ALL-BIG SIX & BIG SEVEN BASKETBALL TEAMS
(As compiled by the Associated Press and United Press)

1940
First Team (Associated Press)
James McNatt, Oklahoma
Ralph Miller, Kansas
Blaine Currence, Missouri
Marvin Mesch, Oklahoma
John Lobsiger, Missouri

Second Team:
Clay Cooper, Missouri
Robert Allen, Kansas
Herbert Scheffler, Oklahoma
Marvin Nash, Missouri
Richard Harp, Kansas

Honorable Mention:
Jack Horacek & Norris Holstrom, Kansas State
Don Ebling, Kansas
Gordon Nicholas & Robert Menze, Iowa State
Sidney Held, Nebraska
Marvin Snodgrass, Oklahoma

1941
First Team (Associated Press)
Howard Engleman, Kansas
Albert Budolfson, Iowa State
Gordon Nicholas, Iowa State
Robert Allen, Kansas
Sidney Held, Nebraska

Second Team:
Chris Langvardt, Kansas State
A.D. Roberts, Oklahoma
Hugh Ford, Oklahoma
Don Fitz, Nebraska

John Kline, Kansas
Honorable Mention:
Martin Nash, Loren Mills & Herbert Gregg, Missouri
Al Randall & John Fitzgibbon, Nebraska
Jack Horacek, Tom Guy & Larry Beaumont, Kansas State
Fred Gordon & Dale DeKoster, Iowa State
Allie Paine, Oklahoma

1942:First Team (Associated Press):
Ralph Miller, Kansas
Albert Budolfson, Iowa State
Gerald Tucker, Oklahoma
Sidney Held, Nebraska
Charles Black, Kansas

Second Team:
A.D. Roberts, Oklahoma
John Buescher, Kansas
Carol Schneider, Iowa State
Ray Evans, Kansas
Bob McCurdy, Oklahoma

Honorable Mention:
Loren Mills, Don Harvey & Herb Gregg, Missouri
Larry Beaumont, Jack Horacek, Bruce Holman, Dan Howe & George Mendenhall, Kansas State
Thomas Hunter & Marvin Sollenberger, Kansas
Richard Reich & Paul Heap, Oklahoma
Robert Harris & Leon Uknes, Iowa State

1947

First Team (Associated Press):
Charlie Black, Kansas
Dick Reich, Oklahoma
Gerald Tucker, Oklahoma (Unanimous)
Dan Pippin, Missouri
Ray Wehde, Iowa State

Second Team:
Harold Howey, Kansas State
Claude Retherford, Nebraska
Otto Schnellbacher, Kansas
Thornton Jenkins, Missouri
Ray Evans, Kansas

Honorable Mention:
Allie Paine, Paul Courty & Jack Landon, Oklahoma
John Rudolph & Darrell Lorrance, Missouri
John Dean, Kansas State
Joe Brown & Rodney Cox, Nebraska
Don Paulsen & Ron Norman, Iowa State

1948

First Team (Associated Press):
Paul Courty, Oklahoma
Thornton Jenkins, Missouri
Clarence Brannum, Kansas State
Howard Shannon, Kansas State
Otto Schnellbacher, Kanas

**Honor Roll
(a new feature of this year's selection):**
Leslie Metzger, Colorado
Ray Wehde and Bob Petersen, Iowa State
Rick Harman and Harold Howey, Kansas State
Dan Pippin, Missouri

Bill Waters, Ken Pryor and Paul Merchant, Oklahoma
Claude Retherford, Nebraska

1949

First Team (Associated Press):
Paul Courty, Oklahoma
Wayne Glasgow, Oklahoma
Claude Retherford, Nebraska
Rick Harman, Kansas State
Bob Rolander, Colorado

Second Team:
Bob Pertersen, Iowa State
Lloyd Krone, Kansas State
Bus Whitehead, Nebraska
Karl Pierpoint, Missouri
Claude Houchin, Kansas

Honorable Mention:
Bill Haynes, Dan Pippin, Don McMillen & Pleasant Smith, Missouri
Clarence Brannum, Ed Head, John Dean & Jack Stone, Kansas State
Bill Waters, Paul Merchant & Ken Pryor, Oklahoma
Don Paulsen & Don Ferguson, Iowa State
Bob Cerv & Joe Malecek, Nebraska
Jerry Waugh & Gene Petersen, Kansas
Bill Ley, Carr Bessemann & Wayne Tucker, Colorado

1949

First Team (United Press):
Rick Harman, Kansas State
Wayne Glasgow, Oklahoma
Milton Whitehead, Nebraska
Claude Retherford, Nebraska
Paul Courty, Oklahoma

Second Team:
Bob Petersen, Iowa State
Claude Houchin, Kansas
Bob Rolander, Colorado
Ken Pyror, Oklahoma
Lloyd Krone, Kansas State

1950
First Team (Associated Press):
Wayne Glasgow, Oklahoma
Kendall Hills, Colorado
Milton Whitehead, Nebraska (unanimous)
Clyde Lovellette, Kansas
Clarence Brannum, Kansas State

Second Team:
Rick Harman, Kansas State
Ernie Barrett, Kansas State
Don Stroot, Missouri
Claude Houchin, Kansas
Lloyd Krone, Kansas State

Honorable Mention:
Paul Merchant, Bill Waters and Wayne Speegle, Oklahoma
Jerry Waugh, Kansas
Don Ferguson and Don Paulsen, Iowa State
Rod Bell, Wayne Tucker and Roger Stokes, Colorado
Bob Cerv, Jim Buchanan, Joe Malecek and Anton Lawry, Nebraska
Bill Stauffer, George Lafferty and Bud Heineman, Missouri
Ed Head and Jack Stone, Kansas State

1951
First Team (Associated Press):
Ernie Barrett, Kansas State
Jack Stone, Kansas State
Lew Hitch, Kansas State
Clyde Lovellette, Kansas

Bill Stauffer, Missouri

Second Team:
Wayne Tucker, Colorado
Bud Heineman, Missouri
Marcus Freiberger, Oklahoma
Robert Pierce, Nebraska
Sy Wilhelmi, Iowa State

Honorable Mention:
Jim Iverson, John Gibson, Dick Knostman, Bob Rousey & Ed Head, Kansas State
George Lafferty & Gene Landolt, Missouri
Bill Houghland & Bob Kenney, Kansas
Gay Anderson & Jim Stange, Iowa State
Frank Gompert, Colorado

1951
First Team (United Press):
Clyde Lovellette, Kansas
Ernie Barrett, Kansas State
Wayne Tucker, Colorado
Lew Hitch, Kansas State
Marcus Freiberger, Oklahoma

Second Team:
Bill Stauffer, Missouri
Jack Stone, Kansas State
Jim Buchanan, Nebraska
Robert Pierce, Nebraska
Sy Wilhelmi, Iowa State

Outstanding sophomore:
Bob Rousey, Kansas State

1952
First Team (Associated Press):
Clyde Lovellette, Kansas
Dick Knostman, Kansas State
Jim Buchanan, Nebraska
Bill Stauffer, Missouri
Bob Kenney, Kansas

Honorable Mention:
 Frank Gompert and Art Bunte, Colorado
 Jim Iverson, Bob Rousey and Jesse Prisock, Kansas State
 Bob Reiter and Gene Landolt, Missouri
 Bill Hougland, Kansas
 Sherman Norton, Oklahoma
 Jim Stange, Iowa State

1952:
United Press not found

1953
First Team (Associated Press):
 Dick Knostman, Kansas State
 Art Bunte, Colorado
 B.H. Born, Kansas
 Del Diercks, Iowa State
 Win Wilfong, Missouri

Second Team:
 Al Kelley, Kansas
 Willard Fagler, Nebraska
 Ron Blue, Oklahoma
 Dean Kelley, Kansas
 Bob Rousey, Kansas State

Honorable Mention:
 Bob Reiter, Missouri
 Fred Seger & Joe Good, Nebraska
 Bob Waller, Oklahoma
 Sam Long, Iowa State
 Gene Stauffer & Gary Bergen, Kansas State
 Harold Patterson & Gil Reich, Kansas
 Frank Gompert, Colorado

1953
First Team (United Press)
 Art Bunte, Colorado
 Del Diercks, Iowa State
 Dick Knostman, Kansas State
 B.H. Born, Kansas
 Al Kelley, Kansas

Second Team:
 Lester Lane, Oklahoma
 Dean Kelley, Kansas
 Bob Rousey, Kansas State
 Fred Seger, Nebraska
 Sam Long, Iowa State

Reference Material

In working on this book, I confined my research to printed newspaper stories about Jack Gardner. I wanted to get as many "views" of Gardner as possible, and that is why I reviewed many newspapers. Each had a particular "slant" to the story and the totality of the reporting has helped me prepare this book. Whether the story was favorable or unfavorable to Gardner meant little to me. I followed the stories wherever they led. All accounts are part of the Jack Gardner story and are related here in **"It's Time To Play!"**

Listed below are the newspapers that I used to reference this book:

Ames Daily Tribune
Boulder (Colorado) Daily Camera
Daily Missoulian (Missoula, Montana)
Dodge City Globe
Great Bend Tribune
Hutchinson News
Hutchinson Herald
Kansas City Star
Kansas City Kansan
Kansas State Collegian
Lawrence Daily Journal-World
Lexington (Kentucky) Herald
Manhattan Mercury
Manhattan Morning Chronicle
Manhattan Republic
Manhattan Tribune
Salina Journal
Seattle Times
Seattle Post Intelligencer
Topeka Daily Capital
University Daily Kansan
Wichita Eagle
Wichita Beacon

The 2006 Kansas State University Basketball Media Guide.

The 2007 Basketball Media Guide for the University of Utah.

Other sources that were valuable in my research:

Championship Basketball with Jack Gardner, by Jack Gardner, 1961 by Prentice-Hall, Inc., Englewood Cliffs, New Jersey.

Aggieville, 1889-1989: 100 years of the Aggieville Tradition, by Dan Walter, 1989. Supplemented and updated in 1995 by Dan Walter.

Sportslaw History: The City College Scandal, sportslawnews.com

Explosion: 1951 Basketball Scandal Threatens College Hoops, by Joe Goldstein, ESPN Classic & ESPN.com.

Profiles of Kansas Hall of Famers, from the Kansas Sports Hall of Fame (kshof.org)

From Playing Field to Battleground: The United States Navy V-5 Pre-flight Program in World War II, by Donald W. Rominger, Jr., Associate Professor of History & Vice President of Student Affairs, East Texas Baptist University, 1985.

The Naismith Memorial Basketball Hall of Fame.

Men's Basketball Championship History from the ncaasports.com

The yearly editions of *The Royal Purple* student yearbook, Kansas State University.

About the Author:

— Courtesy of Joel Klaassen, Hillsboro Free Press

Steven Farney was born and raised in Wilson, Kansas and was a three-year letterman in basketball for the Wilson Dragons. After his senior year, Farney rejected numerous small college basketball scholarships and instead attended Kansas State University as a basketball walk-on. He was among the final cuts in both 1973 and 1974. Scrimmaging against K-State greats Lon Kruger, Chuckie Williams and Mike Evans only increased his desire to play college basketball. In the fall of 1975, he transferred to St. Mary of the Plains College in Dodge City. The 1976 season was a rocky one for the Cavaliers (a record of 6-18) and coaching changes were made. Not wanting to play for another coach, Farney returned to K-State and graduated in 1977 with a degree in History Education.

Music, however, was his first career. Heard singing and playing guitar on the K-State campus, Farney was invited to share his musical talents at St. Isidore's Catholic Church at KSU. From that invitation, he began a 25-year career in church music in parishes across Kansas. Currently living in McPherson, Kansas, Farney has turned to a new career by writing a series of basketball history books about teams and towns, players and coaches in the state of Kansas. His first effort, **"Title Towns: Class BB Boys Basketball Champions of Kansas" (1952-1968)** was released in September, 2006, and has been enthusiastically received. **"Title Towns"** can be found in bookstores across Kansas or on-line at ksheritage.org. **"It's Time to Play!"** is his second book, with more books hopefully to follow.